One Fine Potion

One Fine Potion

The Literary Magic of Harry Potter

Greg Garrett

BAYLOR UNIVERSITY PRESS

DARTON·LONGMAN+TODD

Published in 2010 by
    Baylor University Press
    Waco, Texas 76798-7363

    Darton, Longman and Todd Ltd
    1 Spencer Court
    140-142 Wandsworth High Street
    London SW18 4JJ

Cover Design by Nita Ybarra
Cover image © Shutterstock/Terence Mendoza
Book Design by Diane Smith

Library of Congress Cataloging-in-Publication Data

Garrett, Greg.
One fine potion : the literary magic of Harry Potter / Greg Garrett.
p. cm.
ISBN 978-1-60258-198-2 (pbk. : alk. paper)
1. Rowling, J. K.--Characters--Harry Potter. 2. Potter, Harry
(Fictitious character) 3. Magic in literature. 4. Good and evil in literature.
5. Spirituality in literature. 6. Christianity in literature.
7. Children's stories, English--History and criticism. 8. Fantasy fiction,
English--History and criticism. I. Title.
PR6068.O93Z6735 2010
823'.914--dc22

                                        2010007762

A catalogue record for this book is available from the British Library.
    DLT edition ISBN 978-0-232-52839-8

Printed in the United States of America on acid-free paper with a mini-
mum of 30% pcw recycled content.

THIS BOOK IS FOR ROWAN WILLIAMS

"All good stories change us if we hear them attentively;
the most serious change us radically."

Contents

"If [a myth] works, that is, if it forces us to change our minds and hearts, gives us new hope, and compels us to live more fully, then it is a valid myth."

—Karen Armstrong, *A Short History of Myth*

"True art is moral: it seeks to improve life, not debase it. It seeks to hold off, at least for a while, the twilight of the gods and us. . . . Art is essentially serious and beneficial, a game played against chaos and death, against entropy."

—John Gardner, *On Moral Fiction*

Acknowledgments

This book is a close reading of the Harry Potter novels, but is certainly not the only close reading; it could have been twice as long, although it would hardly have appealed to most general readers at that length. I hope it will spark continued discussion, argument, and appreciation for the deep truths and powerful story so many of us have enjoyed. I owe and acknowledge huge debts to the readers, scholars, theologians, writers, and speakers who helped me make sense of the powerful issues in the Potter books, particularly C. S. Lewis, J. R. R. Tolkien, and N. T. Wright; Barbara Brown Taylor; and Rowan Williams, to whom this book is dedicated. I'm also grateful to the Potter fan community for the incredible amount of information they've made available on the books and on Rowling, and I hope that this book will fill a niche in the Potter community for serious literary, philosophical, and theological discussion of the works.

I thank the Baylor University Press, Carey Newman, director, for asking me to write this book. It's a joy to be publishing a work that will (we hope) bring additional notice to Baylor and to its fine press. Thanks to Elisabeth Wolfe, former student, fine writer and editor, who copyedited this book. Thanks also to those anonymous readers who evaluated my first draft and made comments, many of which I incorporated (and many, perhaps, I should have even if I didn't). I'm grateful to the dean of the College of Arts and Sciences at Baylor, Lee Nordt; to my department chair, Dianna Vitanza, and to my colleagues in the Baylor Department of English for their support and assistance in the work I do as writer. I especially want to thank my friends Tom Hanks, Richard Russell, and Joe Fulton, who model for me daily the joys of the writing and teaching life; and to remember my friend Nancy Chinn, a fine teacher and insightful reader who was, most importantly, a warm, loving, and genuinely good person.

This book was researched and written at Canterbury Cathedral in Canterbury, England; Baylor University in Waco, Texas; Ghost Ranch and the Casa del Sol retreat center in Abiquiu, New Mexico; the National Cathedral, Washington, D.C.; at the Hill Country cabin of my friend Hulitt Gloer outside Kerrville, Texas; and at the Episcopal Seminary of the Southwest in Austin, Texas. At Ghost Ranch I am grateful to Jim Baird, program director; Carole Landess, Casa del Sol host/companion and Debra Hepler, director; at the Seminary of the Southwest, to Alan Gregory, academic dean; John Bennet Waters, chief financial officer; Donald Keeney and the staff of the seminary library; and Stephen Kidd, my research assistant. Parts of this book were researched or written during my Fall 2008 Research Leave from Baylor University, and during my time as Fellow of the Cathedral College of Preachers at the Washington National Cathedral in October of 2008. I remain grateful for both of these opportunities.

I am also grateful to all those places (and the attendant people) where I spoke about or taught the Potter books and films as I was thinking about and writing this book: St. David's Episcopal Church in Austin, Texas; the Episcopal Church of the Good Shepherd in Austin, Texas; Calvary Episcopal Church in Bastrop, Texas; Trinity Episcopal Church in Houston, Texas; Ghost Ranch in Abiquiu, New Mexico; the Society of Biblical Literature in Boston, Massachusetts; the Kino Communales in Stuttgart, Germany; the AmerikaHaus in Munich, Germany; the Episcopal Church Women Triennial at the

Acknowledgments

Episcopal General Convention in Anaheim, California; the Cody Public Library and Christ Episcopal Church, Cody, Wyoming; the Texas Episcopal Church Women in Camp Allen, Texas; and Wesley Seminary, Washington, D.C. Thanks to all those who listened, talked with me about these stories, and shared my interest in reading Harry.

I give thanks for my community of faith, St. David's Episcopal Church in Austin, Texas, for its rector the Rev. David Boyd, and for the Revs. Chad Vaughn, Mary Vano, Ron Smith, Pat Hazel, Cathy Boyd, and Ken Malcolm. I thank my bishop, the Rt. Rev. Andrew Doyle, who supports my work as writer and teacher to the larger church. I thank my friend the Rt. Rev. Greg Rickel, who loves and encourages me in all I do. And I thank my friend Rowan Williams, poet, theologian, father, husband, and exceptional reader, to whom this book is dedicated.

Thanks to my boys, Jake and Chandler, who have shared these stories with me, and to Martha, who puts up with the fractured life of a writer—and, more importantly, with this fractured writer. All three are ongoing evidence in my life of the Deeper Magic.

And finally, my thanks to Joanne Rowling. The story she wrote makes me want to be a better person—which is, I know from experience, just about the best thing you can ever say to a novelist about her work.

Austin, Texas
Epiphany, 2010

Introduction

The Harry Potter Phenomenon

"What do you see when you look in the Mirror?"

—*Harry Potter and the Philosopher's Stone*[1]

Tracking the Boy Who Lived

It was Friday night, July 21, 2007, a hot summer night in Austin, Texas, and my girlfriend Martha and I were sweating, even after the sun went down. Still, I thought as I wiped sweat from my forehead for the fiftieth time, our discomfort couldn't have been much compared to that of my nine-year-old son Chandler, who was clad in a long robe, or, for that matter, to that of any of the others around us wearing robes, cloaks, tall wizard's hats, wigs and false facial hair, and other unseasonal—and unusual—garb. All five thousand of us overheated human beings were milling about in the parking lot of BookPeople, Austin's fine independent bookstore, waiting for midnight, when 1,500 lucky people with book vouchers (including Chandler) were going to take home *Harry Potter and the Deathly Hallows*, the seventh and final book in the Harry Potter series.

As we waited, we were treated to rock music from the Remus Lupins and the Mudbloods, talked to a centaur, watched Chandler

1

participate in a wizard's duel, played wizard games. I was sorted into a Hogwarts house by the Sorting Hat (Gryffindor!). And as we waited, we talked to each other about what we had been waiting for two years to know: Would Harry Potter live? Would he die? Was Snape a villain or a hero? What other beloved characters might be killed in this finale?

These questions were being asked and this scene was being played out, often on a comparably grand scale, across the country— and the sea. My son Jake, who worked at a Barnes & Noble across town, said they were selling 1,000 copies of *Deathly Hallows* at their party. "It's a madhouse," he had told me, which not only mirrored our situation but the situation at bookstores across the U.K. and U.S. on July 21, where 11 million copies of the book would sell within in the first 24 hours of release. Similar hysteria would follow around the world as fans of Harry Potter everywhere from Norway to China sought to get their hands on copies of the book; some would even buy fake versions of *Deathly Hallows*—or badly translated pirate versions—they wanted the book so badly.

But for many of us, wherever we were, although it was rarely spoken as we laughed, played, listened, and waited, we secretly felt anxiety underneath all the excitement and anticipation: Would author J. K. Rowling be able to close her series of books about boy wizard Harry Potter and his friends—the most popular fiction in the history of the planet—in a way that would satisfy us, whether we thought of ourselves as rabid fans, enchanted readers, or grateful teachers and parents? Could she conjure up enough literary magic not only to close the books on Harry, but to write a satisfying coda to a narrative that had entertained, inspired, encouraged, and enlightened fans around the world?

Just before midnight, a bookseller took the stage to announce that we could form into a queue by groups. We were several groups back from the front of the line, and it was around 1 a.m. when we picked up our book. As we tramped back to our car, we had to step over dozens of children and adults who had gotten their books before us and had literally dropped to a convenient spot on the ground and begun reading, often shouting out to each other in excitement or anguish—

"The Death Eaters are going to get him!"

"No they haven't. Keep reading!"

Although it was hours past Chandler's bedtime, I did not force him to go to sleep. He read until 3 a.m., when he nodded off; then I marked his place, took the book from him, and read it myself until I fell asleep.

Over the next few days, many of the people I know asked if I was reading the book.

"Finished," I said, trying not to seem smug. I was too exhausted to be smug.

"Don't tell me," they said, although often they edged a little closer and looked at me with a look you might describe as longing. They wanted to know something, although they also were afraid to know.

I always took pity on these folks, because I would have been exactly in their shoes. So I told them enough: "You'll love it," I said. "It's beautiful. The ending. Perfect. I was blown away. I think you will be too."

Now, we might ask, what makes this anecdote anything more than a reader's memory of a beloved book? Why do so many people have stories about reading Harry, anyway?

These questions matter because J. K. Rowling's Harry Potter series is one of the three most popular literary works in history, outsold to date only by the Bible and Mao's *Little Red Book*. According to Rowling's literary representative, the Christopher Little Literary Agency, as of June 2009, "Well over 400 million copies of the Harry Potter books have been sold worldwide, in over 200 territories and in 67 languages."[2] An entire generation has been raised reading the books, but as *Time* reports, the Potter influence hardly stops with those kids who have grown up reading about Harry. There are also

the 40-somethings, including the President of the United States, who read the books to their children; the 20-somethings whose professors used the case of the Hogwarts House Elves to explicate

3

contract law; the teenagers . . . who were just learning to read when the first novels appears and can now drive themselves to the theater. . . . And then there's the new generation of fans who, rather than having to wait years to find out what happens next, can lock themselves in their rooms for magical marathons and read all 4,100 pages at once or host their own Wizard Film Festival.[3]

In 2000, the editors of the venerable *New York Times* bestseller list, long the gold standard for popularity, decided that they needed to create a children's bestseller list where they could move the Potter books, since the first three were clogging up the main bestseller list and the fourth promised to vault there as well. "The time has come when we need to clear some room," said editor Charles McGrath, justifying the decision.[4] In all, the Potter books spent a decade on the *New York Times* list, one marker of their great popularity. There were, of course, many others: as the Harry Potter phenomenon grew, the release of each book constituted a cultural event marked by (as we have seen) parties, huge crowds, and amazing first-day figures more akin to movie grosses than literary sales: *Harry Potter and The Deathly Hallows* sold 15 million copies worldwide on its first day of release. Indeed, no writer in history has ever enjoyed this sort of success; Rowling is reported by *Forbes* to be the first writer in history to become a billionaire solely through book sales.[5]

They matter as well because English schoolchildren now study *Harry Potter and the Philosopher's Stone* (as the first Potter book was originally published in England and is still known in most of the world) for their A-level exams, and because the books are credited with bringing a generation of American children back to reading. Scholastic, the American publisher of the Potter books, was once perhaps best known for putting on book fairs in schools, but these books made the children's publisher a power in the American market, and the grade school, middle school, and high school students they introduced to reading have continued to look for their next great adventure, perhaps helping to make bestsellers of recent fantasy series by authors such as Rick Riordan and Stephanie Meyer.

They matter because the film series adapted from the books is more popular than either the long-running James Bond films or the *Star Wars* saga. They have helped bring Harry's story, adapted, admittedly, but still largely whole, to millions more who have not read the books. The films too have been media events, with crowds standing in line in costume, and first-day grosses among the highest of all time. *Order of the Phoenix* had an opening day box office of $44.2 million, although *Half-Blood Prince* easily exceeded that, selling over 58 million dollars worth of tickets in the U.S. and Canada on its opening day (and an almost equal amount overseas on that same day), making it the fourth-biggest opening day ever in North America, as well as the top midnight opening in history.[6] As of fall 2009, with *Half-Blood Prince* just gone from theaters and two more films remaining in the series, the films had grossed almost $5 billion worldwide, and *Variety*, the bible of show business, was predicting that the eight-film series could top $7 billion in box office, making it, by some billions, the highest-earning movie series ever.[7]

They matter because the Potter story has spawned a commercial empire, an incredible number of official (and unofficial) products for those fans to consume: board games, Lego building sets, Voldemort replica wands, Gryffindor ties, film calendars, Harry Potter action figures, video games, all elements of a brand estimated by *Forbes* to be worth one billion dollars.[8] In 2010 these Potter products will be joined by The Wizarding World of Harry Potter, an Orlando, Florida, Universal Studios theme park which will recreate a fifteen-story-tall Hogwarts School, the pubs and shops of the Village of Hogsmeade, and the Forbidden Forest at a cost of more than $200 million dollars—and will certainly draw fans from all over the globe.

They matter because literary critics, who normally disdain both children's books and popular fiction—let alone popular children's fiction—have acclaimed the Potter series to a degree that approaches the ridiculous. Not only did the first Potter books (*Philosopher's Stone* and *Chamber of Secrets*) win multiple awards, including the British Book Awards children's book honors, but *Publishers' Weekly*, the bible of the publishing industry, named *Philosopher's Stone* their Book of the Year. Later books won the Hugo (science fiction's

5

greatest honor), the British Book Awards Book of the Year, and *Newsweek*'s Best Book of the Year. While some critics (including Harold Bloom) and authors (including Ursula LeGuin and A.S. Byatt) complain that the books are derivative or somehow don't measure up as literary works, other writers, including Stephen King, Salman Rushdie, and me (in my novelist's guise), have extolled them.

They matter because no other contemporary story has been more read, watched, discussed, and lived than this narrative. A huge international fan community has grown up around the books: top Web sites like Muggle Net and The Leaky Cauldron have invested thousands of human-hours into gathering info and news on the Potter books and films, and are visited by tens of millions of people from all over the world; Harrypotterfanfiction.com, for example, contains over 50,000 fan-written narratives set in J. K. Rowling's universe and claims over 40 million hits per month, and other sites boast even more Potter fan fiction.[9] In the intervals between books—and since all the books have appeared—fans joined online and in person at conferences like Leaky Con in Boston, Terminus in Chicago, and Azkatraz in San Francisco to celebrate, talk about, and act out the books that have so entertained and shaped them. (Oh, yes—and to dance. As reported in *Time*, "wizard rock" or "wrock" bands playing songs derived from the Potter novels and sporting names like Harry and the Potters, the Remus Lupins, the Whomping Willows, and DJ Luna Lovegood have become an international phenomenon, "playing at conventions and clubs and wizard-rock festivals," and demonstrating yet more examples of a passionate Potter fan community that seems to have taken on a life of its own as a full-fledged cultural movement.)[10] The books have now all been released; the movie story is almost done; but the community that has grown up around Harry Potter seems to be going strong, thanks for asking.

Clearly these novels have involved people like few stories in history. From a literary standpoint, we might explain that Rowling creates compelling characters and a world where magic is possible, dragons breathe flame, and giants stomp, but she is hardly the first to do this, or even to do it well; she does, however, join the elite

6

club of writers of powerful fantasy or "children's" tales such as C. S. Lewis and J. R. R. Tolkien whose works are read by children and teens, and then reread by them, often throughout their lives. As Lewis noted in his role as literary critic, when a book is powerful enough to not only be read but reread, then those who return to it must be gaining something more than mere excitement; since rereaders already know what is going to happen to Harry, whether or not Hagrid or Hermione will survive, clearly rereaders come back to Potter for compelling reasons besides a compelling story.[11]

Lewis, writer, literary critic, and friend to other writers, gave the experience of reading a great deal of thought. He concluded that in truly great stories, while we might be engaged by the events of the story, the plot was merely a net to catch something else, and that what winds up entangled in the net—even if only for the space of several chapters—represents our real reasons for reading.[12] What is in the net? Well, just as Dumbledore left (admittedly, with some ulterior motives) Hermione Granger his copy of *Tales of Beedle the Bard* "*in the hope that she will find it entertaining and instructive,*" Lewis tells us that we read tales to "see with other eyes . . . imagine with other imaginations . . . feel with other hearts, as well as our own."[13] In great stories we are both entertained and edified, and we learn things about ourselves, others, and the world that we might not otherwise have known. Great stories, like Harry Potter's, teach us as well as entertain us, and this enlightenment may also encourage us to become people more like those we behold in the stories we read.

So finally, we might say that the Harry Potter books matter because of their artful telling—and retelling—of powerful and potent stories about human life. In the pages of Rowling's books, we learn about the use and misuse of power, about the necessity of community, about heroism and villainy, and about hope for a brighter future. By walking alongside Harry, Ron, and Hermione, we are able to participate in an adventure that sheds light on our own adventure, if we have eyes to see and ears to hear.

To explore those stories, we will be employing an ancient method of reading used in the Middle Ages to read the Bible, and suggested by the poet Dante as a useful way to read all great books: the four-fold method of Thomas Aquinas and other great medieval scholars. While many good readers are aware that they are seeking something in addition to an engaging story when they approach a narrative, not many readers could explain how their reading leads them to consider deeper questions inspired by the story; so you'll understand precisely how I'm arriving at the conclusions I reach, I want to explain the four-fold method, a time-tested approach to consider all that a good book has to offer us. When we read a book, we begin, of course, at the *literal* level of story, the words and narrative that must be understood as literature and in the context of their culture. We read also on an *allegorical* level, seeking the deeper philosophical and spiritual themes embodied in the work. We read on a *tropological* level as well, paying attention to the themes that might impel us to greater insight and action, making a work a part of ourselves. And finally, we read on the *anagogical* level, a reading that pays attention to themes of transcendence and hope for the future. The goal of all of this reading—which doesn't have to occur in this exact sequence or even with this degree of formality—is to bring the work to life within you, which Lewis and fellow literary critic Northrop Frye would agree is the purpose of a good reading of any great book, opening up possibilities for us to gain wisdom, insight, and even transformation.[14] In this book we will focus on one primary way of reading in each chapter, moving from a literal understanding of the place of magic in the Potter novels in chapter 1, then to a consideration of the theme of community in chapter 2, then to the call to action issued by the books in chapter 3, and finally to a spiritual and even religious understanding of the future given us by the books and by Rowling's own beliefs in the final chapter. You need not share those beliefs (or read the final chapter, for that matter) to observe how the Harry Potter tale shares many resemblances to Christian faith and practice, but I think our reading of the books would be incomplete without that observance.

Since J. K. Rowling is a classicist who has sprinkled the Potter novels with Latin, clad her characters in medieval robes, and educated them in castles, a medieval way of reading not only seems fitting but—as I hope this work demonstrates—is a terrific method for discerning C. S. Lewis' "something more" in the story of The Boy Who Lived. Rowling has created a world where we can be entertained, inspired, and enlightened. In an exciting tale of magic, heroes, and villains, she has also shared wisdom about power, and suggested that everything in the world she has created is undergirded by a deeper magic. In the pages that follow, we shall see how the reaction of characters to that deeper magic, their choices to draw closer to it or flee from it (for choice, as Dumbledore knew and often said, is at the heart of who we are and what we become) map out the borders of J. K. Rowling's epic. In the hands of the gifted author who has created this living world, we can experience again (or for the first time) truths and insights about human life— who we are, why we are here, where we should be going—that offer us a glimpse of joy.

And the gleam of something beyond.

1

Platform 9¾

Magic, Power, and the Fantastic

"Harry Potter was a wizard."

—*Harry Potter and the Chamber of Secrets*

"Lord Voldemort showed me how wrong I was. There is no good and evil, there is only power, and those too weak to seek it."

—Professor Quirrell,
Harry Potter and the Philosopher's Stone

Harry Potter, Gateway to Evil

J. K. Rowling tells a story about an encounter she had in the early years of Harry Potter in New York City; she was in the FAO Schwarz toy store buying gifts for her daughter, when a particular kind of religious man leaned in close to her and spoke. "He said, 'I'm praying for you,'" she remembered, "in tones that were more appropriate to saying 'Burn in hell.'"[1] While this anonymous man never explained his grievance to her, there's little doubt what that grievance was— like many others objecting to the Potter books, he was most probably concerned about the presence of magic in the stories, since in his worldview magic was necessarily dark, a thing of evil.

From the beginning, Harry Potter could not step out of 4 Privet Drive without being accompanied by controversy; for a decade now, the Harry Potter books have been attacked by conservative cultural and religious figures as works promoting witchcraft, Satanism, and antisocial behavior. In 2000 a widely circulated email message spread across the Internet, claiming the book was itself a gateway to black magic:

> Harry Potter is the creation of a former UK English teacher who promotes witchcraft and Satanism. Harry is a 13 year old "wizard." Her creation openly blasphemes Jesus and God and promotes sorcery, seeking revenge upon anyone who upsets them by giving you examples (even the sources with authors and titles!) of spells, rituals, and demonic powers. It is the doorway for children to enter the Dark Side of evil. . . .

To support these contentions, the "author" of the email had collected several stories of children who had read and been led astray by the books, among them the case of "dear Ashley,"

12

> a 9-year-old, the typical average age reader of Harry Potter: "I used to believe in what they taught us at Sunday School," said Ashley, conjuring up an ancient spell to summon Cerebus, the three-headed hound of hell. "But the Harry Potter books showed me that magic is real, something I can learn and use right now, and that the Bible is nothing but boring lies."[2]

This e-mail, as has been widely noted in print and Web urban legend publications, actually drew its "facts" from an article in the humor publication The Onion (facts such as "dear Ashley," the child inspired and somehow enabled to summon Cerberus the three-headed dog by reading *Harry Potter and the Sorcerer's Stone*), but even after discovering that they had mistakenly quoted a satirical news source that was itself poking fun at Harry Potter hysteria, many opponents of the Potter books said that although that particular source might be bogus, their claims were nonetheless true.[3]

Although Harry has gotten on the wrong side of all sorts of religious and cultural battles, much of the negative has come from conservative Christians. These believers argue that the Harry Potter saga is bad for children because it contains and promotes witchcraft, and the Bible is explicit in its condemnation of witchcraft. To evangelical Christians and others encouraged to read the Bible literally as a record of God's unchanging message to humanity, there seems to be little wiggle room in the way the Bible, particularly the Old Testament, talks about sorcery. Leviticus commands, "You will not practise divination or magic" (Lev 19:23b, NJB). The book of Deuteronomy goes into more detail in its command to eschew magic:

> When you have entered the country given you by Yahweh your God, you must not learn to imitate the detestable practices of the nations there already.
>
> There must never be anyone among you who makes his son or daughter pass through the fire of sacrifice, who practises divination, who is soothsayer, augur or sorcerer, weaver of spells, consulter of ghosts or mediums, or necromancer.
>
> For anyone who does these things is detestable to Yahweh your God; it is because of these detestable practices that Yahweh your God is driving out these nations before you. (18:9-12, NJB)

The rejection of sorcery remains a dogma in the Christian church today, particularly observed among Catholics and evangelicals, and it is from these quarters that many of the strongest condemnations of Harry Potter have emerged. An exorcist at the Vatican recently attacked the Potter novels for their use of magic, calling "fictional wizard-in-training Harry Potter the 'king of darkness, the devil.'"[4] Pope Benedict himself has spoken out against the Potter novels on several occasions. Most recently, in January 2008, the pope argued that Harry's stories were a dark mirror image of the *Lord of the Rings* and *Narnia* stories, often celebrated by Christians. Like other critics, Pope Benedict argues that the Potter books lead children to an "unhealthy interest" in Satanism, and concludes that "despite several positive values that can be found in the story, at the foundations of this tale is the proposal that of witchcraft as positive, the violent manipulation of things and people thanks to the knowledge of the occult, an advantage of a select few."[5]

13

Similar criticisms of the Potter novels have also come from Greek Orthodox Christians, and from other religious traditions, especially from conservative Muslims, who argue that the depiction of magic and the supernatural in the book is "contrary to Islamic values."[6] The Potter books were banned from schools in the United Arab Emirates, have been attacked by a state-run newspaper in Iran, were pulled from some Muslim schools in Britain because of fundamentalist protests, and have perhaps even been the object of terrorism; in Pakistan in August, 2007, a bomb threat postponed the launch of *Deathly Hallows* at a book store in Pakistan, and police suspect that the threat emerged from religious objections to the Potter books.

And while other religious people (including me) have praised the books for their imagination, the moral values of their heroes, the strong contrast between good and evil, and their similarities to faith narratives (including, in its review of the film version of *Half-Blood Prince*, the same Vatican newspaper that had previously condemned the books), others continue to denounce them in the strongest possible terms.[7] In addition to those recent comments from the pope, Dr. James Dobson, founder of Focus on the Family, released this correction in 2007 when a press account suggested he approved of the Potter books:

> "We have spoken out strongly against all of the Harry Potter products." [Dobson's] rationale for that statement: Magical characters—witches, wizards, ghosts, goblins, werewolves, poltergeists and so on—fill the Harry Potter stories, and given the trend toward witchcraft and New Age ideology in the larger culture, it's difficult to ignore the effects such stories (albeit imaginary) might have on young, impressionable minds.[8]

Following Rowling's post-*Hallows* announcement that Dumbledore was gay, the Christian Coalition and Pat Robertson's Christian Broadcasting Network, which had previously ridden the fence on the Potter books, condemned them strongly. A guest on CBN, Jack Roper, took the opportunity to use the Dumbledore controversy to return to the roots of the argument: "As a cult researcher for many years, I have seen contemporary witchcraft packaged in many seductive forms, and Harry Potter is the best."[9] One needs only look at the comments section of any Christian Web site publishing a positive assessment of the Potter books to discover that a vocal segment of the faithful still consider the books Satanic, evil, and a negative influence on anyone who reads them. Some have even suggested that they—and books like them—could lead to such horrific violence as the Columbine shootings; when once we invite evil into our schools, they say, who knows where it will stop?

One of those arguing that the Potter books' use of magic actually infected classrooms with evil was anti-Potter activist Laura Mallory, the Georgia housewife who received worldwide attention for her attempts to have the Potter books pulled from her child's school; I first read about her in the London *Daily Mail.* When the school refused, she went to the Georgia Board of Education, then petitioned the state Superior Court, where at last her legal options ended, although her passion did not diminish. Melissa Anelli, Webmistress of the Potter fansite The Leaky Cauldron, went to Georgia to interview Mallory, expecting to find someone who was deranged or paranoid; how could someone claim that God had told her not to read these books that had meant so much to so many?

But Anelli said that what she discovered in Laura Mallory was resolute sincerity and confidence that she was right: "[Harry] is a wizard. Witchcraft is evil . . . one day everyone will know that witchcraft is evil."[10] Mallory's reading of Harry Potter told her that it was primarily about magic, and her interpretation of the Bible taught her that witchcraft—even fictional witchcraft—was an affront to God, and she could not be shaken from that belief. Laura Mallory, and people who believe as she does, cannot be argued with; Anelli certainly tried. But when you consider that this fear of witchcraft grows out of the very real belief that people of goodwill are matched in spiritual warfare with dark forces, then perhaps these sorts of misconceptions and misunderstandings become more understandable, if not excusable. One should not be afraid of a fictional wizard—and the books are, as Rowling insisted, deeply moral. But this continuing controversy has made it possible for the Potter novels to be simultaneously the most-read fiction in history and, according

15

to the American Library Association, the most-banned books of the twenty-first century.[11]

Perhaps the great irony of Dr. James Dobson, the pope, and Muslim fundamentalists finding common ground around their condemnation of J. K. Rowling's works as leading to an unhealthy interest in the occult is that since her earliest interviews about the controversy, Rowling has categorically denied any such intent or content. As far back as 2000 on the *Today Show* with Katie Couric, Rowling had this very clear response to a viewer's question about witchcraft and Satanism:

> **Katie Couric:** Tammy in Kansas was wondering: "What would encourage you to write books for children that are supporting the devil, witchcraft and anything that has to do with Satan?" You've heard that before.
>
> **J. K. Rowling:** Well, nothing would encourage me to do that because I haven't done it so far so why would I start doing it now?
>
> **Katie Couric:** You have heard criticism along those lines ever since the beginning, and I think it also grew since more and more books came out.
>
> **J. K. Rowling:** A very famous writer once said: "A book is like a mirror. If a fool looks in, you can't expect a genius to look out." People tend to find in books what they want to find, and I think my books are very moral. I know they have absolutely nothing to do with what this lady's writing about.[12]

So it is also, perhaps, ironic after chronicling the ongoing contention to suggest that this fuss is primarily the result of bad reading. Rowling's use of magic as an element in her stories is simply a convention of the fantasy and fairy-tale genres and not actually about faith and belief, but rather about power and the willingness to use it. In this chapter, we will explore the world of magic, considering the criticism that Rowling sets up magic as a belief system or presents a Gnostic view of reality in which the magical world and its practitioners are somehow superior to magicless Muggles. And in the process, we will consider the idea that magic is simply an

16

ingredient in the type of story Rowling has chosen to tell, and one that speaks more about our misplaced human desire for power than about any supernatural powers of evil.

Magic and the Two Worlds

Magic and Muggles are opposed elements of the Potter story, and it can be easy to misunderstand what Rowling intends to do by creating this contrast. In the course of the Potter narrative, we meet first the horrid Dursleys of 4 Privet Drive, who glory in their suburban normalcy, who have kept Harry under their thumbs for eleven years, and who will continue to make Harry's life a living hell. They are the most Mugglesome of Muggles, "perfectly normal, thank you very much" non-magic people who want no surprises, no changes, and no drama in their lives—except for the drama they themselves create.[13] Vernon Dursley, director of a drill-making firm, is perpetually apoplectic; on the day before his nephew Harry Potter comes to live with them, he "yelled at five different people. He made several important telephone calls and shouted a bit more. He was in a very good mood."[14]

In that first chapter of *The Philosopher's Stone*, we also make the acquaintances of representatives of the Wizarding world: Albus Dumbledore, the headmaster of Hogwarts School of Witchcraft and Wizardry, Harry's future mentor and friend; and Minerva McGonagall, his future teacher and house head, who can't believe Dumbledore truly intends to leave Harry with his non-magical and thoroughly unpleasant aunt and uncle. The two friends are in shock, grieving the great loss of Lily and James Potter amidst the euphoria at the defeat of Lord Voldemort. Then, out of the night, a third representative of the magical world, Hagrid, the Hogwarts gamekeeper, comes roaring in with baby Harry astride Sirius Black's motorbike. Before he gives over the child to be left on the Dursleys' doorstep, he kisses the baby, and grief as outsized as he is boils over at the idea of leaving this child of wizards here in Little Whinging. "S-s-sorry," sobbed Hagrid . . . "But I can't stand it—Lily and James dead—an poor little Harry off ter live with Muggles—"[15]

17

A simplistic division of Harry's life into two distinct worlds—Wizarding and Muggle—is part of the misconception of those who believe that magic is the defining element of the Potter stories. In this misreading, there are two worlds, the mundane and the magical, and Harry is an orphan and a misfit in one world but a hero in the other. Certainly one could read the books this way—their beginnings and endings, typically set in non-magical England, show a Harry deeply unhappy at being where he is, while his adventures and acclaim come, at least in the earlier books, entirely in the Wizarding world at Hogwarts School of Witchcraft and Wizardry. This simplistic division between worlds does break down somewhat in later books, however. In *Goblet of Fire*, Harry's great battle with a revived Voldemort occurs in a Muggle graveyard, far from Hogwarts; in *The Order of the Phoenix*, Harry and his cousin Dudley are attacked by Dementors in suburban Little Whinging; in *Deathly Hallows*, Harry, Hermione, and Ron have adventures the length and breadth of the United Kingdom (including a pivotal scene in the Forest of Dean, where Rowling grew up) and return to Hogwarts only for the climactic battle against Voldemort and the Death Eaters. That battle, of course, changes the game for everyone, wizards and Muggles alike; Voldemort is a threat to the entire world.

If we are to read the Potter novels first on a literal level and to place them in an understandable context, then magic is the essential element with which we need to grapple. Are the books *about* magic? Magic pervades the books, certainly, and it would be easy to read them literally and simply assume this. But careful reading suggests an alternative: any simplistic division of Harry's life into two realms, one of which is assumed to be superior to the other because of its possession of magic, crashes against one of Rowling's most obvious concerns, that of tolerance. The Wizarding world, as will see, is no Utopia; it is only superior to the Muggle world in magic and magical artifacts. It does not surpass the Muggle world in compassion, tolerance, or love; although we have no major Muggle characters who are not Dursleys, we never imagine that Hermione Granger's parents love any less than Ron

Weasley's parents do, and conversely, the wizards living in the Wizarding world clearly show that they are no more unified or universally compassionate than those living in the Muggle world. Both "worlds" are disturbingly, hopefully human.

Therefore the notion that wizards and the "reality" they inhabit are somehow superior sounds like an exposition of Grindelwald's, Voldemort's, or Lucius Malfoy's most prejudiced ideas—that magic-using humans are elevated above those who cannot use magic or those magical races who somehow differ from them. As Rowling noted, this reading of the books is in direct conflict with the narrative itself, which dramatically illustrates the evil of prejudice: "Bigotry is probably the thing I detest most. All forms of intolerance, the whole idea of 'that which is different from me is necessarily evil.' . . . This world of witches and wizards, they've already ostracized, and then within themselves, they've formed a loathsome pecking order."[16] Two worlds exist, true, but only the villainous characters in either would pretend that their world is superior.

Those who attack the Potter novels as "Gnostic" are probably referring to two distinct aspects of that philosophical and even religious idea: the belief that true salvation comes from secret knowledge held by an elite group, and the concept that there are two realities, with the one we live in being only a shadow of a higher and greater realm. There is, to be truthful, a great deal of secret knowledge in the Potter novels; wizards learn spells and incantations, and since the Statute of Secrecy, they have hidden themselves, their magic, and all magical creatures away from the Muggles. Wizards themselves are secret knowledge. They make this choice, however, not because they inhabit a different world, but because they inhabit the same world, and their secrecy is not simply about preserving secret knowledge; it also serves to protect them—and Muggles—and to preserve the status quo. Hagrid explains to Harry that the Ministry of Magic hides their existence from the country because, "Blimey, Harry, everyone'd be wantin' magic solutions to their problems."[17] And of course as we (and they) remember from the past, fear-filled Muggles do have a penchant for burning the occasional suspected magic-user at the stake. Even if, according to Wizarding history,

19

they tend to burn the wrong people and not to harm the actual witches and warlocks, why stir up such alarm and loathing?

The idea that there are two realities, one more "real" than the other, is an ancient idea, emerging in Greek philosophy, and in religious belief going back at least to the Manichaeans in the first few centuries C.E. It is also a modern idea, found among many religious fundamentalists of various faith traditions who insist that the world we inhabit is completely fallen, and merely a shadow of the true spiritual reality to come. Alister McGrath describes this belief espoused by the Manichaeans as "a fundamental tension between the spiritual realm (which is seen as being good) and the material realm (which is seen as being evil)."[18] One could regard the Wizarding world as a spiritual realm, since much is hidden from the eyes of Muggles, and certainly some wizards believe that they occupy a higher plane of existence. This is the justification used by Voldemort and the Death Eaters to kill Muggles for sport, or by Grindelwald (and the young Albus Dumbledore) to rule over Muggles for "the greater good," as they once plotted together.

20   So if we believe arguments that Muggles are inferior to wizards, then perhaps this radical division of reality makes sense. Certainly Voldemort believes it. At the outset of *Goblet of Fire*, he claims to the caretaker who discovers him in his father's old house that he is not a human (despite his human birth): "I am not a man, Muggle," said the cold voice . . . "I am much much more than a man."[19] However, the wizards we most admire in the story—the adult Dumbledore, Arthur Weasley, and others—argue that there is no difference between wizards and Muggles. As with the Jews so reviled by German Nazis, there is no physiological difference between oppressor and oppressed. In Book 7, future Minister of Magic Kingsley Shacklebolt exhorts listeners of the *Potterwatch* broadcast to shelter Muggles from the Dark Lord and his minions by casting protective spells over their dwellings, and concludes, "We're all humans, aren't we? Every human life is worth the same, and worth saving."[20]

Ultimately wizards and Muggles are both human beings, with different gifts; one might have a gene for magic, another a gene for music. But there is no biological distinction between Muggle and magic-user—just prejudice (on both sides) about superficial differences. Just as Harry does not occupy a higher world because of specialized knowledge, he is not somehow superior to the non-Wizarding population because he can cast an "Expelliarmus" charm. Rowling brings these understandings to life for us in a number of ways. First, while Harry's discovery that he is a wizard delights him, becoming a part of the Wizarding community and mastering secret knowledge does not bring him peace or joy in and of itself; it is not a key to redemption or to a higher being. In fact, in some ways, Harry's life for seven years is constantly complicated and endangered because of his knowledge of this other world, and his mastery of magic is not at the core of who he is or even at the heart of his final victory over Voldemort. As Stephen Fry observed to an agreeing Rowling onstage at a talk at the Royal Albert Hall, "It's desperately important that the way Harry solves all his problems is really through his courage, his friendship, and his loyalty and stoutness of heart."[21] Secret knowledge or inhabiting a higher reality do not constitute Harry's redemption; instead, as we will explore in chapter 2, it is the very human joys of love, companionship, and community that give his life meaning.

Second, Rowling draws so many correspondences between the Wizarding world and the Muggle world that there can be little question that she sees them simply as two sides of the same coin, two experiences of the same reality. From the outset of the saga, it seems clear, for example, that the Wizarding world is as full of bad people as is the mundane world, something Rowling demonstrates for us from the beginning of Harry's journey. While the Dursleys are indeed horrible—"You couldn't find two people who are less like us," as Minerva McGonagall says, describing them and their already horrifying little boy—Rowling doesn't mean to suggest that they (and Muggles in general) are uniquely horrible.[22]

There are terrible people in both worlds; the first representative of the Wizarding world that Harry meets (after Hagrid, of course) is Draco Malfoy, who is directly compared to Harry's horrid Muggle cousin: "Harry was strongly reminded of Dudley."[23] Likewise we see

21

Malfoy early in *Chamber of Secrets,* when Harry observes him from a hiding place in Flourish and Blotts, the dark magic store that Harry has entered accidentally. Draco is dragged into the store by his father Lucius, and he behaves precisely as we have seen Dudley behave, sulking, whining, and saying, "I thought you were going to buy me a present."[24] These two boys, Dudley and Draco, are presented as twin bullies, Harry's chief antagonists in the world of his childhood, tormenting him at each of his homes, and they are presented as mirror images so that we might understand that there is no fundamental difference between them.

Draco, who will be a part of Harry's life from their first introduction on, also previews in their first meeting an important element of the Wizarding world which will grow in importance throughout the saga, the completely human bigotry and intolerance of wizards. When Harry meets Draco in Madam Malkin's robe shop, Draco inquires whether Harry's parents were "*our* kind," and lets drop that he doesn't believe "they should let the other sort in" to Hogwarts.[25] Rowling intended to plant this focus on Wizardly racism and intolerance from the outset: "It was always there from the beginning, as you saw with Draco—even from [the] first book with Draco Harry discovers him being rude about Muggles."[26]

It is Draco and his family who will carry the banner of "pure-bloods" versus "Mudbloods" and "blood traitors" until Voldemort returns to do it himself, and it is Draco who first utters the insult "Mudblood" to Hermione Granger, although she and Harry need to have it explained to them by Ron: "Mudblood's a really foul name for someone who is Muggle-born—you know, non-magic parents. There are some wizards—like Malfoy's family—who think they're better than everyone else because they're what people call pure-blood. . . . It's a disgusting thing to call someone."[27]

In the eyes of the Malfoys and the other Death Eaters, and in Voldemort's own self-loathing prejudice, Muggles are inferior, but even among those in the magical world there are gradations of acceptability, "us" and "them," just as there have always been prejudices in the world you and I inhabit. Wizards who call themselves pure-blooded set themselves up as superior to those who are of

22

mixed blood, or who have no magical abilities at all, just as people have always divided themselves by blood or by race or by culture. These distinctions, though, as Voldemort's own Muggle ancestry suggests, are spurious. As Dumbledore once wrote Lucius Malfoy, explaining a decision not to pull a Muggle-sympathizing story in the *Tales of Beedle the Bard* from the library, there are no purely magical families: "So-called pure-blood families maintain their alleged purity by disowning, banishing, or lying about Muggles or Muggle-borns on their family trees. They then attempt to foist their hypocrisy upon the rest of us by asking us to ban works dealing with the truths they deny. There is not a witch or wizard in existence whose blood has not mingled with that of Muggles."[28]

Muggles and so-called pure-bloods are no different, and their worlds are likewise no different. That the magical world is not, in and of itself, intended to be a separate or superior realm may be demonstrated finally by referring to the first chapter of *Harry Potter and the Half-Blood Prince*, when the Muggle Prime Minister is visited by Cornelius Fudge, "The Other Minister," and the Prime Minister tries to express the difficulties of his present moment, only to be brought up short by Fudge:

> "Difficult to know where to begin," muttered Fudge, pulling up the chair, sitting down, and placing his green bowler hat upon his knees. "What a week, what a week. . . ."
>
> "Had a bad one too, have you?" asked the Prime Minister stiffly, hoping to convey by this that he had quite enough on his plate already without any extra helpings from Fudge.
>
> "Yes, of course," said Fudge, rubbing his eyes wearily and looking morosely at the Prime Minister. "I've been having the same week you have, Prime Minister. The Brockdale Bridge . . . the Bones and Vance murders . . . not to mention the ruckus in the West Country."[29]

It seems clear that these leaders occupy the same world, not separate ones, that they struggle with the same challenges although they come at the experience from different directions. Voldemort's rise to power menaces both worlds, Muggle and Wizarding alike, as the film of *Half-Blood Prince* demonstrates dramatically with its Death

Eater attacks on the Millennium Bridge, a well-known London tourist attraction, rather than the fictional Brockdale Bridge.

The Prime Minister imagines that because wizards "can do *magic!*" they should be able to sort out anything, but as Fudge and new Minister of Magic Rufus Scrimgeour tell the Prime Minister when they depart his office by flue, magic does not solve all problems, particularly when one's enemies also possess it (any more than, to draw an analogy, nuclear weaponry solves all geopolitical problems for those who control it). It is simply a tool to be used.[30] What matters, ultimately, is not whether one has a magic wand or an M-16: it is what one chooses to do in response to the circumstances of one's birth and upbringing, and the company one finds oneself in because of one's choices. As Fry said with Rowling's assent, the books are less about casting spells that they are about power, what one does with it, with whom, to whom.

Perhaps, finally, the only real difference between the Wizarding world and the Muggle world may be reflected in the type of "magic" people employ to exercise power. Wizards are those who, through an accident of birth, possess some innate mastery of spells; Muggles have developed technology—cars, batteries, escalators, and many other devices—to the great astonishment of Arthur Weasley: "*'Fascinating!'* he would say as Harry talked him through using a telephone. '*Ingenious*, really, how many ways Muggles have found of getting along without magic.'"[31] Other wizards also seem to find Muggle technology estimable. In Book 7, for example, Dedalus Diggle makes much of Uncle Vernon's ability to drive: "Very clever of you, sir, very clever, I personally would be utterly bamboozled by all those buttons and knobs," and he is hardly the only wizard to view technology as something fantastic and barely believable.[32]

All this simply goes to remind of us of the familiar rule formulated by science fiction author Arthur C. Clarke: "Any sufficiently advanced technology is indistinguishable from magic." Just as Sirius is said by the Muggles to be armed with a gun, "a kind of metal wand that Muggles use to kill each other," J. R. R. Tolkien also suggested that there was ultimately little difference between magic and technology.[33] He spoke of the mechanisms used in a world

24

(real or fictional) to project power, whether mechanical, magical, or personal, as "The Machine," and said there was little difference between these methods when they were employed for "the corrupted motive of dominating: bulldozing the real world, coercing other wills."[34] In other words, Hitler's Blitzkrieg of tanks and Stukas is indistinguishable from Voldemort's volley of dark curses; magicians and Muggles alike employ power, but while wizards have magic wands, charms, and brooms, Muggles have electricity and the plugs and batteries so beloved by Mr. Weasley, who finds them magical. Both are "secret knowledge" to the uninitiated; neither makes for a "superior reality."

The Unforgiveable Curses

When Voldemort launches the Second Wizarding War, all his dark magic (and that of his followers) is marshaled to attain one goal: power. He wants power over others, and ultimately power over death, and magic is his tool in those quests. By eliminating his enemies (including, most especially, Harry) and by taking control of the Wizarding community, Voldemort will be unchallenged and will then be able to exert his will over the non-magical Muggles and other wizards as he desires. His pursuit of a certain powerful magic wand—what we know to be the Elder Wand—in *Deathly Hallows* is in service to these goals; if somehow Harry's wand has stymied Voldemort's every plan to destroy him, then the Dark Lord will simply need to employ a more powerful wand.

Voldemort's followers likewise hope to attain power through the ascent of the Dark Lord; as Voldemort asks the Malfoys after taking over their manor, "Is my return, my rise to power, not the very thing [you] professed to desire for so many years?"[35] This desire is precisely the sort of thing that Augustine was referring to many years ago when he spoke of what he called the disordered desires of human beings; although we desire things strongly, often they are the wrong things, harmful to ourselves and others. More recently, Dr. Martin Luther King Jr. has said that "Much of the evil which we experience is caused by man's folly and ignorance and also by the misuse of his freedom."[36] Dumbledore would, in all likelihood,

25

have concurred with both men: toward the end of his life, he wrote of "The Tale of the Three Brothers" that "the quest for the Elder Wand merely supports an observation I have had occasion to make over the course of my long life, that humans have a knack of choosing precisely those things that are worst for them."[37] For the Malfoys, particularly, their disordered desire for wealth and power leads them to the brink of destruction, for their support of the Dark Lord in pursuit of their goals is almost their undoing, and only too late do they discover that what they care about most of all is not wealth or power but each other.

Those who employ dark magic are traditionally those who most strongly exhibit a will to power; as Harry learns early, most dark wizards have arisen from Slytherin, of whom the Sorting Hat sang, "Those cunning folk use any means / To achieve their ends."[38] However, in their education at Hogwarts, all students are supposed to learn to control their magic and not to use it in ways that are proscribed by the Wizarding community. At the orphanage, for example, Dumbledore says to Tom Riddle (who even this early has been using his power to torment and frighten others):

> At Hogwarts . . . we teach you not only to use magic, but to control it. You have—inadvertently I'm sure—been using your powers in a way that is neither taught nor tolerated at our school. You are not the first, nor will you be the last, to allow your magic to run away with you. But you should know that Hogwarts can expel students, and the Ministry of Magic . . . will punish lawbreakers most severely.[39]

At Hogwarts and in the Wizarding world at large, there are legitimate uses of magic; it is a tool to be harnessed. It can be used to do daily chores or even to explore the mysteries of the cosmos, but to those of evil inclination, magic becomes something more, a tool for imposing their will upon others, and it is upon this use that the Ministry necessarily sets boundaries.

Many types of magic are regulated by the Ministry of Magic: underaged wizards are not allowed to cast spells; magic-users are not permitted to attack Muggles with their spells or to allow non-magical persons to see them performing magic; and Arthur

Weasley is constantly chasing after pranksters who subject Muggles to shrinking door keys and biting kettles and the like. But only three curses are classified as Unforgiveable Curses, and these illegal curses can explain a great deal about the use of magic to project personal power. Certainly the Wizarding community treats these spells as most serious violations; the impostor masquerading as Alastor Moody explains in his Defense Against the Dark Arts class in *Goblet of Fire*, "The use of any one of them on a fellow human being is enough to earn a life sentence in Azkaban."[40] These three curses all represent the most onerous magical projections of one's power onto another, and so we might say that the Imperius Curse, the Cruciatus Curse, and *Avada Kedavra* are magic at its darkest and most dangerous.

The Imperius Curse is a mind-control curse; as "Moody" demonstrates in the classroom, he can order his Imperiused spider to do anything he wishes: swing as though on a trapeze, do a back flip, do a cartwheel, tap dance. The students laugh at this show, but "Moody" is unsmiling. "'Think it's funny, do you?' he growled. 'You'd like it, would you, if I did it to you?'"[41] They wouldn't like it, of course; since the Imperius Curse allows the caster to impose her or his will on the one so cursed, one of the qualities that we hold to be most distinctly human, that of free will, is taken away. The Imperius Curse is rightly condemned, for a successful curse does what not even the most totalitarian regime could ever accomplish: it takes away the option of dissent, hidden though it might be.

Harry and his classmates learn that it is possible to fight the Imperius Curse with one's own will, and Harry proves to be remarkably good at it. But as "Moody" points out, throwing off the Imperius Curse "takes real strength of character, and not everyone's got it."[42] For many in the Potter novels, being Imperiused is a sentence of involuntary servitude that goes on and on, under which they may do many things they would not wish to do. A prime example is in Book 7 when, under the Imperius Curse, Ministry officials are forced to help overthrow the Ministry. When you can force people to act against both their own desires and their own best interests, then you have absolute—if reprehensible—power over them.

27

The Cruciatus Curse is another means by which the evil wizard imposes his or her will on another. Victims of the torture curse may be induced to act in a certain way or to give information, but the curse can also be used to influence those who may be forced to witness the curse. Harry and Ron would do almost anything rather than listen to Hermione as she is tortured by Bellatrix Lestrange in *Deathly Hallows*, and what parent, lover, or friend could easily stand by as a loved one is subjected to such pain? The Cruciatus Curse also has the potential to drive a recipient insane; Bellatrix tortured Neville Longbottom's parents to madness in the First Wizarding War, and that threat of permanent disability adds to the menace of the spell. Torture is defined as the imposition of pain on another, whether to punish, to force speech or action, or for the personal pleasure of the torturer. Whatever the case, it is also an imposition of power on the powerless worthy of its status as unforgiveable.

Finally, the ultimate power is not simply to compel or to harm; it is to destroy, and *Avada Kadavra*, the Killing Curse, gives one that power. The spell is not identified until Book 4, when Hermione answers "Moody"'s question about the final Unforgiveable Curse, but we see it in action earlier in *Goblet of Fire*. It is the Killing Curse, of course, that murders the Riddles at their table, the ancient crime of which Muggle gardener Frank Bryce is suspected, and the flash of green light which follows the words Lord Voldemort speaks inside the old Riddle house shows us that it is *Avada Kedavra* that the Dark Lord employs to kill Frank as well. This is, as "Moody" says, the "last and worst" spell, but it requires "a powerful bit of magic behind it—you could all get your wands out now and point them at me and say the words, and I doubt I'd get so much as a nosebleed."[43] Real malice, real evil, and real ambition are needed to harness this spell, of which Harry is the lone survivor in Wizarding history.

These three spells are the ultimate examples in Harry Potter of what Tolkien referred to as The Machine, manifestations of magic that the powerful use to impose their will on the less powerful. But we should not make the mistake of Professor Quirrell, who believed that power was all that matters; Rowling makes it clear that there are such things as good and evil and that use of magic to impose

28

one's power over another is, most definitely, the latter. That is why, after Snape and the Death Eaters take over the school, the changes at Hogwarts are so alarming and contrast so sharply with the reasons Hogwarts has always existed. When Neville tells Harry and the others that Defense Against the Dark Arts is now simply called the Dark Arts, and that students are expected to practice the Cruciatus Curse against their classmates when they are given detentions, we can see that the focus of the school—to teach people to use their magical powers wisely and with respect—has been lost. Power has won out over the notion of good and evil.

Use of any of these curses—ever—is an evil act, and when asked, Rowling has not tried to defend Harry, who employs them on several occasions. At the end of *Order of the Phoenix*, for example, Harry launches the Cruciatus Curse at Bellatrix Lestrange, escaping from her murder of Sirius Black. It knocks Bellatrix off her feet, but she teaches him that—as "Moody" had noted of the Killing Curse— simply mouthing the words does not carry the force of the spell: "You need to *mean* them, Potter! You need to really want to cause pain—to enjoy it—righteous anger won't hurt me for long."[44] Harry attempts the Cruciatus Curse again—twice in *Half-Blood Prince*, when Snape and Draco Malfoy are escaping Hogwarts after Dumbledore's death—and casts it with some success in *Deathly Hallows* at Amycus Carrow after Carrow spits in Professor McGonagall's face. In that novel, Harry also finds himself forced to use the Imperius Curse in Gringott's to control the goblin Bogrod and Death Eater Travers, although he confesses that he hasn't cast it well and has to recast it on both, and Professor McGonagall also uses the Imperius Curse in *Deathly Hallows* against Carrow.

Clearly, even good people can be tempted—or feel the need in these situations—to exercise power over others, and the power that Harry does possess, the power of love, hardly seems equal to the task of protecting him or overthrowing the Dark Lord. But Harry's awareness that some spells are good and some evil is clear despite his occasional failings, and never is it more clear than when he casts an unknown spell—*Sectumsempra*—on Draco Malfoy in *Half-Blood Prince*. Instantly, Malfoy is stricken:

29

Blood spurted from Malfoy's face and chest as though he had been slashed with an invisible sword. He staggered backward and collapsed onto the waterlogged floor with a great splash, his wand falling from his limp right hand.

"No—" gasped Harry.

Slipping and staggering, Harry got to his feet and plunged toward Malfoy, whose face was now shining scarlet, his white hands scrabbling at his blood-soaked chest.

"No—I didn't—"

Harry did not know what he was saying; he fell to his knees beside Malfoy, who was shaking uncontrollably in a pool of his own blood.[45]

Harry is appalled at the force he has unleashed with this unknown spell, which Snape angrily identifies as dark magic. "I'm not defending what I did," Harry later tells Hermione. "I wish I hadn't done it. . . . You know I wouldn't have used a spell like that, not even on Malfoy."[46] The film of *Half-Blood Prince* dramatically suggests Harry's remorse by showing him slumped, overcome by emotion, in reaction to Draco's suffering, and by his agreement to get rid of the Half-Blood Prince's potion book, the one from which he took this dangerous spell; in the novel, he hides the Prince's textbook in the Room of Requirement so as to keep it out of Snape's hands but does not dispose of it. But in both cases, Harry knows that what he has done—this power he has attempted to exert over another, even his enemy—is wrong. While, in the heat of emotion, Harry sometimes reacts to provocation by using magic in an evil fashion, there is no suggestion that these misuses of power are acceptable because it is Harry doing them. Rather, as Rowling pointed out, they are reminders that Harry is simply human—and reminders to us all to be on our guard lest we too find ourselves attempting to control, harm, or destroy those with whom we are at odds through the power we have at our disposal.

Magic and the Fantastic

J. R. R. Tolkien recognized that the equation of magic with power was a simple one to make; in his own *Lord of the Rings* saga, he related how Rings of Power—magic rings made with the aid of Sauron, the Dark Lord of his mythos—came into being, and how in his tale, power was an "ominous and sinister word" when applied to anyone except the very gods themselves. In Tolkien's fantasy world, magic could easily become corrupted into evil because of the desire for power, something common to stories of this type.[47] J. K. Rowling's choice of a particular mode of narrative—the children's story, subset fantasy literature—means that she too naturally incorporates a number of traditional story elements. In Harry Potter, the world is filled to overflowing with magical creatures—dragons, gnomes, sphinxes, unicorns, werewolves, giants, and more besides—and with magic of all sorts. Wizards can vanish and reappear, turn teacups into gerbils, transform themselves—or others—into animals. In Rowling's world, wizard-brewed potions can bring good luck or love (or the illusion of it) or cause instant death. Swords, necklaces, journals, and wands can bear fantastic charms or perform powerful magic. Magic is a central—and typical—part of these books, although that does not mean that magic is the point of them.

Fantastic tales have often used this backdrop of magic, and have often conveyed powerful mythic and spiritual meanings in this context. So it is that, before we turn our attention to the way the Harry Potter books deal with life in community, good and evil, heroism, and hope, we will conclude our consideration of magic by discussing the fantasy genre in which Rowling set her tales. Although she writes about a world in which magic is possible and supernatural creatures roam, her characters wrestle, as all of us must, with very human emotions, decisions, fears, and desires. In all of this we can see similarities to classic fairy tales, such as Rowling mimicked in creating *The Tales of Beedle the Bard*, and to fantasy epics such as those written by J. R. R. Tolkien, C. S. Lewis, and others.

In composing the Harry Potter story as a work of children's fantasy, Rowling wrote novels that, as Lisa Miller suggested in *Newsweek*, were new entries into the distinguished tradition of British fantasy, a tradition that cannot seem to help dealing with ultimate questions.[48] As G. K. Chesterton famously said, literature of the fantastic can be moral without moralizing, and this has always been a

31

valuable trait of fantastic literature, whether written for children or enjoyed by all ages. In the Potter novels, Rowling speaks and writes about tolerance; her moral passions do emerge in her writing. So although converting readers is not her aim, in the context of her seven-volume fairy tale, she clearly has issues she wants to explore, and her beliefs have filtered into the way she treats the primary themes of the Potter epic: heroism, sacrifice, community, tolerance, faith. In this, we discover that Rowling is very much like Lewis, who once spoke of how in writing fantasy, one can bring truth to life again by stealing past the "watchful dragons" of piety and convention.[49] (Compare the motto of Hogwarts School of Witchcraft and Wizardry, which contains, as Rowling has said, very practical wisdom, but might also be an account of how stories might work: "*Draco dormiens nunquam titillandus*," that is, "Never tickle a sleeping dragon," or "Let sleeping dragons lie.")

Part of this truth-telling comes because of a tale's mythic quality. Myth has long been recognized as vital in its retelling of ancient stories and ability to convey wisdom. As Karen Armstrong points out, ancient peoples understood the world in two primary ways, *mythos* and *logos*, and both were regarded as attempts to convey the truth about reality. One, *logos*, was empirical and could be verified by observation, but the other, *mythos*, was considered to be equally concerned with truth even though that truth could not be demonstrated by rational means. "Myth," Armstrong says, "was not concerned with practical matters, but with meaning. Unless we find some significance in our lives, we mortal men and women fall very easily into despair. The *mythos* of a society provided people with a context that made sense of their day-to-day lives; it directed their attention to the eternal."[50] Myth helps us make sense of all the aspects of our lives.

While modern life has privileged the fact-based form of knowing, both rational and imaginative understanding are essential. The Scottish fantasy writer George MacDonald acknowledged that perhaps "'the facts of Nature are to be discovered only by observation and experiment.' True. . . . We yield you your facts. The laws we claim for the prophetic imagination. 'He has set the world *in* man's

32

heart,' not in his understanding. And the heart must open the door to the understanding."[51] The imagination looks beyond the factual and makes it possible for us to gain some understanding of even those things that are beyond proof. Within the context of a story—even a story filled with the seemingly impossible—we too can be redirected and retaught who we are and what should matter to us, and this moral instruction comes in a way that is fresh and vital because it steals past the dragons. As Lewis said in a review of Tolkien's *Lord of the Rings* saga, "The value of myth is that it takes all the things we know and restores to them the rich significance which has been hidden by 'the veil of familiarity.'"[52]

So it is that in the guise of a story like Harry Potter's, we too can sidestep the veil of familiarity and see the mythic truths again through new eyes. It is essential for our moral development, Stanley Hauerwas argues, "to be introduced to stories that provide a way to locate ourselves in relation to others, our society, the universe." Such stories of moral location, he says, will of necessity be "adventures, for there is no self devoid of adventure."[53] We need adventure to see the shape of a life, but sometimes it can be difficult to see that shape in the adventures of the everyday; while my moral self may be revealed by my quest to finish my grocery shopping, might it not shine out even more clearly if I were trying to get through a dark and magical forest, beset by dangers? In the great fantasy stories of MacDonald, Lewis, and Tolkien, we at once remove ourselves from reality and, as my colleague Ralph Wood notes in his book on Tolkien, are enabled to escape into reality.[54]

The fantastic worlds of magic, combat, and supernatural creatures present the illusion that we are not concerned with the events of the day-to-day, what Armstrong described as one of the primary functions of myth. Yet by the time we conclude our reading, we are often surprised at the way great works of fantastic literature can teach us about our own lives and beliefs. In *The Lord of the Rings*, for example, Tolkien tested Frodo, his hero, to his limits and beyond, and yet, miraculously, all was well: as Tolkien noted, Frodo's "sufferings were rewarded by the highest honour; and his exercise of patience and mercy toward Gollum gained him Mercy."[55]

33

Rowling subjected Harry to tasks that would seem to be beyond anyone, let alone a single teenaged boy, and yet he constantly reaffirmed for us the virtues of love, compassion, and unselfishness. In these fantastic adventures, we can experience these vital human qualities ourselves. Thanks to J. K. Rowling's work, we can gain wisdom and understanding about the hard business of being human.

At the same time, as these examples suggest, amid stories marked by great horror, difficulty, and death, fairy tales and tales of the fantastic often direct us, paradoxically, toward hope, commitment, and life. Foes of fairy tales throughout the ages have condemned them as violent, dark, and bloody and said that while they may be written for children, children should by no means read them. Rowling has had her share of these complaints, particularly as the books (in the minds of some critics) grew ever more dark and violent.[56] But Rowling (in the guise of Albus Dumbledore) responds to these critics by pointing out that fairy tales have always been dark, that it is a vital part of their allure and their function. Dumbledore's commentary to the old wizarding tale "The Wizard and the Hopping Pot" mentions the bowdlerizing witch Beatrix Bloxam, who condemned fairy tales such as those in *The Tales of Beedle the Bard* for "their unhealthy preoccupation with the most horrid subjects, such as death, disease, bloodshed, wicked magic, unwholesome characters, and bodily effusions and eruptions of the most disgusting kind." Like many Muggles over the years, in response and outrage, Bloxam wrote versions of these same tales that eliminated any such elements—and any real-world relevance— so that, as Dumbledore notes, Bloxam's "tales" have evoked only a negative response from all those who read them: "uncontrollable retching, followed by an immediate demand to have the book taken from them and mashed into pulp."[57]

This uncontrollable retching is a response to unacceptable sweetness. Tales that are not honest about death, disease, bloodshed, wicked magic, and the like are, first, untrue. However noble the motives for removing ugliness from art, even art intended for children, it is not representative of life. And leaving death out of the story—even a children's story—may be avoiding one's artistic responsibility. J. R. R. Tolkien wrote in his seminal essay "On Fairy-Stories" that while fantastic literature offers escape from the hustle and bustle of modern life, "there are other things more grim and terrible to fly from . . . . There are hunger, thirst, poverty, pain, sorrow, injustice, death." In words that might remind us of *Deathly Hallows* and, more particularly, Voldemort's soul-shaping compulsion, Tolkien goes on to say that "the oldest and deepest desire" is "the Great Escape, the Escape from Death."[58] So to write a tale in which—whatever Beatrix Bloxam might say—death is never threatened is to fail as a storyteller who desires both to entertain and be honest. In Rowling's own words, failing to engage death is to fail to engage life: "The real master of Death accepts that he must die, and that there are much worse things in the world of the living. It is not about striving for immortality, but accepting mortality."[59] The responsible author of any work—including fairy or children's tales—must acknowledge this truth.

Moreover, to leave out ultimate crises is to destroy the dramatic potential for those happy endings so usual and so necessary to fairy tales. Tolkien spoke approvingly of "the Consolation of the Happy Ending," and argued that all complete fairy tales must end happily. However true tragedy might be as drama, the fairy tale calls for the precise opposite; Tolkien (as was his wont) actually coined a word to describe the effect we expect at the end of a well-rendered fantastic tale: *Eucatastrophe* ("*Eu*" comes from the Greek prefix for "good," and marks a reversal or transformation of the disastrous events which have gone before). "The eucatastrophic tale," Tolkien said, is the truest fairy tale, and in it we see "its highest function."[60] Thus in a tale where we come to the point of disaster—and then see that disaster somehow miraculously or magically reversed—we are brought to believe that such reversals are possible, right, and just.

Magic in a fantastic story seems to mark a world as somehow unlike our own, putting us at our ease as we read that we are not dealing with our own problems, and thus luring us into engagement with the ideas and issues that emerge from the narrative. As in other fantasy novels and tales, magic in Harry Potter is not a belief system, nor in Rowling's imagination does it delineate a separate, superior world. So in these novels, while magic may be an accepted part of the world, as we've discovered, it is not the point of the world; magic is used in the same sorts of way that we in our world might use science and technology, for good or ill. A responsible reading of the element of magic in Harry Potter shows us that ultimately it is about power—how it is employed, and how it should not be employed. Harry is fortunate to be surrounded by a community of friends and classmates who can help do the work for which Dumbledore suggested Hogwarts exists, that of teaching wizards what is and is not an acceptable use of power. It is in community that we find ourselves, understand our missions, and seek real meaning, and so it is to community and communion that we will turn next in exploring deeper meanings in Harry Potter.

The Order of the Phoenix

Community, Diversity, and Formation

"Harry had no one."

—*Harry Potter and the Philosopher's Stone*

"We're with you whatever happens," said Ron.

—*Harry Potter and the Half-Blood Prince*

Community and Compassion

I have never yet passed through King's Cross Station in London when I haven't seen people (often a great seething lump of humanity) gathered to get their pictures taken at Platform 9¾, where a luggage trolley (or, to be a prosaic Muggle, part of one) sticks out of a brick wall, something like the very brick we might imagine Harry and his Hogwarts colleagues passing through to board the Hogwarts Express. While I have not taken my turn trying to pass through the wall, I will confess that I have more than once wished that it were possible to cast a discreet jinx on someone or that I had access to a Time Turner to add just a few more hours to my next deadline. Although I think we've settled that magic in the Harry Potter books is not intended as an alternative belief system or the sign of a higher reality, magic is at the heart of the appeal to many readers of the saga—and likewise, as we've seen, at the heart of the fear of those who worry about their influence.

But whether Harry Potter rides a broom, drives a car, or steers a spaceship, his story is at its center about a boy who did not know where he came from and found home, a boy who so loved the community he became a part of that he willingly gave his life for it. The books bear only Harry Potter's name, and it is he, The Chosen One, The Boy Who Lived, whose life occupies the center of each of the novels. Each book bears the name of a different adventure—*The Prisoner of Azkaban*, *The Goblet of Fire*—but they are all part of one grand adventure, the adventure of a person finding home and entering community, of a person discovering where he belongs—and with whom. In this dramatic exploration of the importance of community in the novels, we find a subject ripe for our second level of reading, the allegorical, where we seek to find philosophical or spiritual meaning, wisdom with which to live our lives.

When our saga begins, Harry is an orphan who believes himself to be—and, for all intents and purposes, is—alone in the world. Is there a more heartbreaking line in modern fiction than the one from *Sorcerer's Stone* prompted by his first letter from Hogwarts: "No one, ever, in his whole life, had written to him"?[1] Harry is unloved by his nearest relatives, who shut him away in a cupboard under the stairs; he is friendless at school because his cousin Dudley and his gang despise him: "At school, Harry had no one. Everybody knew that Dudley's gang hated that odd Harry Potter in his baggy old clothes and broken glasses."[2] It's an aching loneliness, one that Harry feels will never lift. And yet, during the course of his story, he meets those who are his fellows, who become a new family to him, who shape him, who uphold him in all he does, and finally, who make it possible for him to do the great work to which he is called. Ultimately, Harry makes possible a world where old divisions are erased, old lines blurred, and a larger, more inclusive community can form—

And all of this has surprisingly little to do with magic. If Platform 9¾ is symbolic in some way, what is most important about it is not the idea of magic that draws people to gather there, but those people gathered, the Muggles like you and me in the station now—and the Hogwarts students and families in Harry's story. In one of the first serious discussions of the Potter books, Alan Jacobs wrote that the purpose of Hogwarts is not just to teach students how to use magic (the technical aspects of spell casting, potion-making, etc.), but to teach "the moral discernment necessary to avoid the continued reproduction" of dark wizards like Voldemort.[3]

We have already seen Dumbledore speak of how he hoped that Hogwarts would shape Tom Riddle, not simply how he would be taught to use magic; a primary purpose of communities like Hogwarts School of Witchcraft and Wizardry is to develop character. In reading the books, we follow Harry through seven years of education and formation, both formal and informal. It is for this reason that Harry's story is sometimes referred to by literary critics as a *Bildungsroman*, the traditional literary term for a story about the education of a young person. "It is Harry's journey," Rowling says of the saga she wrote, and what matters most in the course of the story is how Harry learns from encounters, people, and his own successes and failures to become a worthy person—a person capable of doing what is right.[4] Much of that moral discernment comes in response to those in Harry's life—family, friends, and the communities to which he belongs, either by accident or by choice.

Love, friendship, tolerance, and family are all central themes of the Harry Potter story, and all revolve around our relationships with others. Rowling clearly thinks these are vital; not only did she foreground these thematic elements in the Potter tale, but in her commencement address at Harvard, Rowling discussed imagination (in the sense of empathy and compassion with others) and friendship as the two pieces of wisdom she wished to pass on to those best and brightest. The focus on friendship, compassion, and empathy supports a powerful wisdom reading of the Potter novels, for one of the great spiritual truths is that we must recognize the importance and validity of others.

Compassion and concern for one's fellow human beings seem to be universally extolled among the great wisdom traditions. In

Buddhism, this understanding is found in the centrality of compassion for all life; four of the Five Noble Precepts of Buddhism revolve around respectful relationship with others (and the fifth, which is to avoid intoxication, could also be interpreted in light of our treatment of others). One of the Five Pillars of Islam is *Jakat*: all good Muslims are called to share of their possessions with those who are in need, and this act of turning toward another is considered to be as important as the action of turning toward Mecca in daily prayer. Within the Jewish tradition, the Rabbi Hillel, a contemporary of Jesus, told a seeker who wanted a summary of the Jewish Law, "What is hateful to yourself, do not do to your fellow man. That is the whole of the Torah and the remainder is but commentary." Hillel's version of what we now call the Golden Rule—treat others as you yourself wish to be treated—is one of many such formulations from many different cultures. Charles Kimball suggests that this clear requirement is at the heart of all wisdom traditions that are "authentic, healthy, life-sustaining."[5] Other versions, spoken by Jesus, Confucius, or Socrates, to name a few, show us that compassion and empathy are at the heart of any transformational spiritual understanding.

Rowling herself has talked about how empathy is essential for human beings on a journey, and we see it expressed dramatically in her stories. Hermione, particularly, is a person capable of seeing and feeling the suffering of others. When at the beginning of *Order of the Phoenix* Harry has, by Dumbledore's orders, been left alone with the Dursleys all one miserable summer and angrily takes his friends to task when he sees them again, his angry resentment and bitter speech would call up defensiveness and indignation in many of us. But Hermione listens to him rant and then responds, "'Harry, we're really sorry!' . . . 'You're absolutely right, Harry—I'd be furious if it was me!'"[6] It is Hermione who recognizes that "Professor Moody"'s demonstration of the Cruciatus Curse on the spider is disturbing Neville (whose parents, we later learn, were tortured by the self-same spell) and who—fine student though she is—actually interrupts the lesson:

"Stop it!" Hermione said shrilly.

Harry looked around at her. She was looking, not at the spider, but at Neville, and Harry, following her gaze, saw that Neville's hands were clenched upon the desk in front of him, his knuckles white, his eyes wide and horrified.[7]

Hermione later rushes Ron and Harry out of the class, not to go to the library, as Ron suspects, but to check on Neville, who they find standing frozen in the middle of the hallway, "staring at the stone wall opposite him with the same horrified, wide-eyed look he had worn when Moody had demonstrated the Cruciatus Curse."[8] Although Hermione speaks gently to him, he's clearly strongly affected by what he has witnessed—emotions to which Harry and Ron have been oblivious.

And in contrast to almost all the other characters, who respond with revulsion and disgust to Kreacher, Hermione joins Dumbledore in showing sympathy to the ancient house elf who has imbibed the vile blood theories and evil of the House of Black. Even though Kreacher reviles her as "Mudblood" and recoils from her touch, Hermione can imagine his lot and his life, even understanding why he might have betrayed his master Sirius Black to Sirius' cousins Narcissa Malfoy and Bellatrix Lestrange:

41

> "Harry, Kreacher doesn't think like that," said Hermione, wiping her eyes on the back of her hand. "He's a slave; house-elves are used to bad, even brutal treatment. . . . He's loyal to people who are kind to him, and Mrs. Black must have been, and Regulus certainly was, so he served them willingly and parroted their beliefs. . . . Sirius was horrible to Kreacher, Harry . . . Kreacher had been alone for a long time when Sirius came to live here, and he was probably starving for a bit of affection. I'm sure 'Miss Cissy' and 'Miss Bella' were perfectly lovely to Kreacher when he turned up, so he did them a favor and told them everything they wanted to know."[9]

Hermione is one of Rowling's characters who displays the compassion and empathy that truly good people are supposed to demonstrate; Dumbledore is another. More centrally, of course, Harry learns these qualities, embraces them, and becomes a sacrificial hero who gives his life for the people he loves. Voldemort doesn't have these qualities and, what's more, doesn't ever want them, and he is destroyed—physically and spiritually—because he fails to see the importance of communion. But other villains besides Voldemort result from the human failure to see our common humanity; there are also real world villains, as J. K. Rowling knows better than most of us. During her time working at Amnesty International, she encountered the broken victims of power-hungry people, but she also saw the power of human good: "The power of human empathy, leading to collective action, saves lives and frees prisoners. . . . Unlike any other creature on this planet, humans can learn and understand, without having experiences," she said in her speech at Harvard. This ability to empathize, she went on, was more than just a gift; it was a responsibility. Refusing to empathize with others might not mean that the person cutting her- or himself off would personally become a monster, she noted, but it certainly made the actions of actual monsters possible.[10] The failure of people of good will to understand the needs of those who suffer ultimately leads to as much damage as the active evil of those who exploit them, for without that empathy, how can anyone be engaged to care?

Compassion means more than simply kindness to the weak and downtrodden, however, although in almost all wisdom traditions it certainly means that. It also means loving and attempting to understand those who oppose us, those who share our humanity if not our opinions. This is a countercultural and perhaps even a counterintuitive action, but it is at the heart of compassion teachings. In surprising ways, the Potter novels also show us unaccountable mercies rendered to others—even to those we might think of as aliens or enemies. Dumbledore's willingness to offer people a second chance (one of his defining characteristics, according to Hagrid), Hermione's concern for all creatures including goblins and house elves, Harry's mercy extended to Peter Pettigrew when Sirius and Lupin intend to kill him in *Prisoner of Azkaban*, Harry's rescue of his longtime enemy Draco Malfoy from the blazing Room of Missing Things in *Deathly Hallows*, and even Harry's concern for the mewling naked fetus that is the remnant of Voldemort's soul in the ethereal King's Cross Station at the end of *Deathly Hallows* are strong reminders that we are called to be in relationship with others, to recognize the needs of others, and to forgive others, even when they are different or difficult.

Rowling has said, in fact, that one of Harry's defining characteristics is that he is a person who rescues others, even when it is inconvenient or dangerous or even—as in the case with Voldemort's maimed soul—counterproductive. "Harry's impulse, to the point of utter wrongheadedness," Rowling said, "is to save. His deepest nature is to try and save, even when he's wrong to do so, when he's led into traps . . . now he goes off and tries to save as many people as he can."[11] Harry even offers Voldemort one last chance to repent—to feel remorse—although the Dark Lord disdainfully refuses it, and goes on to his own doom:

> "I'd advise you to think about what you've done. . . . Think, and try for some remorse, Riddle. . . ." . . . "It's your one last chance," said Harry. "It's all you've got left. . . . I've seen what you'll become otherwise. . . . Be a man . . . try . . . Try for some remorse. . . ."[12]

By "be a man," Harry means that Voldemort should put away his notions of being more than human, as he had told the Muggle caretaker, and to embrace his humanity, with all the responsibility that comes with it. To be truly human is to be a person who cares for others, although this is unfortunately something Voldemort will never do, and it is the end of him. Being unable to imagine and care about the lives of others not only leaves him spiritually void, it also leaves him blinded to the way others think, feel, and react—and results in his physical death as well.

Community and Formation

But being in community is about more than what we are able to do for others; we are also formed in community, educated and supported and challenged to reach our fullest potential as human beings. Dumbledore had hoped that Tom Riddle might find himself

transformed from a selfish and dangerous boy into a more responsible man by the Hogwarts experience; certainly this is what happens to Harry Potter, another orphan who comes to Hogwarts.
Harry fulfills his destiny only through his interactions within that
community, and he is ultimately pointed toward and strengthened
to become his best and most noble self in and through others. He
learns formally from his teachers, even those he hates, like Snape
(perhaps especially from Snape, by the time the series is concluded);
he learns informally from Ron, Hermione, Neville, and Luna. When
we consider the Harry Potter story start to finish, we discover that it
is the story of how an orphan finds a family; how a boy alone winds
up surrounded by people who love, support, and follow him; and
how a group of people comes together to become a community with
sufficient virtue to stand up for the truth even when it means facing
death. These are powerful truths worth carrying into our own lives.

Since we are made for community, it is with great sadness that
we recognize that when we first meet him, Harry Potter's essential
condition is that of isolation, a condition that recurs with some
frequency throughout Harry's story. Although he discovers friends
and a sort of family in the Wizarding world, Harry is also, by virtue
of who he is and what he is called to do, lonely for much of his life.
We see this isolation most strongly in *Order of the Phoenix*. When
Dumbledore pulls away from Harry for fear of inducing Voldemort
to exploit the connection between himself and the boy, when most
people in the Wizarding world refuse to believe Harry's version of
his encounter with Voldemort and Cedric Diggory's death at the
conclusion of *Goblet of Fire*, and when even close friends such as
his roommate Seamus pull away from him or question his veracity,
Harry is left in a fearful state of solitude. The film version of *Order
of the Phoenix* finds a wonderful way to express this theme visually
in shots of Harry alone, and in a new scene between Harry and Luna
Lovegood placed early in the film:

> **Luna Lovegood:** [about her father] We believe you, by the way.
> That He-Who-Must-Not-Be-Named is back, and you fought him,
> and the Ministry and the Prophet are conspiring against you and
> Dumbledore.

Harry Potter: Thanks. Seems you're about the only ones that do.

Luna Lovegood: I don't think that's true. But I suppose that's how he wants you to feel.

Harry Potter: What do you mean?

Luna Lovegood: Well if I were You-Know-Who, I'd want you to feel cut off from everyone else. Because if it's just you alone you're not as much of a threat.

There are many times in the novels when Harry feels completely alone, abandoned, misunderstood. In *Order of the Phoenix,* he lashes out at his friends after being left alone all summer, and after Sirius' death at the Ministry of Magic, Harry pushes back even against Dumbledore. The headmaster, who loved Sirius and Harry alike, and who has lost more than a few people he loved to death, tells Harry that he knows how he must be feeling, but Harry cannot see beyond his own intense pain: "'YOU DON'T KNOW HOW I FEEL!'" Harry roared. "'YOU—STANDING THERE—YOU—'"[13] In that moment, Harry again feels as though he is alone in the universe. Through the love and patience of Dumbledore, Hermione and Ron, and Hagrid, however, he is reminded that he is part of a community, but he still cannot help but feel separate in some ways, particularly after he hears about the prophecy from Dumbledore:

> Perhaps the reason he wanted to be alone was because he had felt isolated from everybody since his talk with Dumbledore. An invisible barrier separated him from the rest of the world. He was—he had always been—a marked man. . . . It was sunny, and the grounds around him were full of laughing people, and even though he felt as distant from them as though he belonged to a different race, it was still very hard to believe. . . .[14]

When we study Harry's loneliness and the importance of community in relieving it, we also gain new understanding of the Dark Lord's brokenness. Voldemort's essential state of solitude is self-chosen; to love others or to be part of a larger community are the furthest things from his mind. The closest he will ever come to community is to create Horcruxes, fragments of his own self, a

45

horrid parody of community that Voldemort hopes will spare him from the fate of all humankind—and from any need for it. Like Jean Paul Sartre, perhaps, Voldemort would opine that Hell is other people.

C. S. Lewis explores this idea in his novel *The Great Divorce*, where he actually depicts Hell as a great gray city, its interior largely depopulated. Its inhabitants have all moved out farther and farther into the suburbs because they can't bear to be in contact with anyone. "They've been moving on and on," a character on the bus tells the novel's narrator. "Getting farther apart. They're so far off by now that they could never think of coming to the bus stop at all. . . . Millions of miles from us and from one another. Every now and then they move further."[15] Voldemort would perhaps be happy out in the suburbs of Hell, if only because he would have no need for or contact with others, but for those of us who are called to community, distance and nonengagement are not options.

Voldemort does not understand—in fact, denigrates—love, but Dumbledore has long recognized that strength is to be found only in that deeper magic. It is Dumbledore who forms the two iterations of the Order of the Phoenix; it is in his honor that his students name their student magic class Dumbledore's Army; and it is the headmaster who constantly insists that Harry include his bosom friends Ron and Hermione in the difficult and dangerous adventures thrust upon him, as in the beginning of *Half-Blood Prince*, when Harry admits he has not told anyone about the contents of the prophecy about him. Dumbledore approves his reticence, but then urges him to relax his discipline "in favor of your friends":

> "I think they ought to know. You do them a disservice by not confiding something this important to them."
>
> "I didn't want—"
>
> "—to worry or frighten them?" said Dumbledore, surveying Harry over the top of his half-moon spectacles. "Or perhaps, to confess that you yourself are worried and frightened? You need your friends, Harry. As you so rightly said, Sirius would not have wanted you to shut yourself away."[16]

Sirius, who loved and needed his friends, is a good model for Harry, for when Sirius disregarded his friends and struck out on his own, disaster often followed.

We need others, as we are reminded throughout the Potter series, although our tendency often is to draw away from others or, even worse, to voluntarily divide ourselves. Witness the song of the Sorting Hat in *Order of the Phoenix*, the beginning of the first Hogwarts year following Voldemort's return. After noting the historic conflict between the Hogwarts founders and the departure of Slytherin, the Sorting Hat goes on to sing,

> And never since the founders four
> Were whittled down to three
> Have the Houses been united
> As they once were meant to be.
> And now the Sorting Hat is here
> And you all know the score:
> I sort you into houses
> Because this is what I'm for,
> But this year I'll go further,
> Listen closely to my song:
> Though condemned I am to split you
> Still I worry that it's wrong, . . .
> Still I wonder whether sorting
> May not bring the end I fear.[17]

47

By setting ourselves apart, whether it is in failing to confide in others or segregating ourselves from others, we make hells for ourselves—and cut ourselves off from becoming who we are supposed to be.

It is within family that we first hope to encounter community, and it is there that we hope to have our emotional and formational needs met. When families work right, we find a soothing similarity—Leo Tolstoy began the novel *Anna Karenina* by saying that "Happy families are all alike." But, as in Harry Potter's story, family can and sometimes does fall short of acting as a loving and supportive community. Henri Nouwen noted that in many families, "love comes in a very broken and limited way. It can be tainted by power plays, jealousy, resentment, vindictiveness, and even abuse. . . . Sometimes human love is so imperfect that we can hardly recognize it as love," which seems an apt description of life at 4 Privet Drive.[18]

One would hardly recognize what the Dursleys have given Harry as "love." Dumbledore sums up Harry's existence with Uncle Vernon and Aunt Petunia in Book 6:

> "You have never treated Harry as a son. He has known nothing but neglect and often cruelty at your hands. The best that can be said is that he has at least escaped the appalling damage you have inflicted upon the unfortunate boy sitting between you [Dudley]. . . . However miserable [Harry] has been here, however unwelcome, however badly treated, you have at least, grudgingly, allowed him houseroom."[19]

Although the Dursleys are related to Harry by blood, they have failed him, and Barbara Brown Taylor observes that, unfortunately, "Many families do not work right. They are not schools in forbearance and forgiveness but reformatories where rules are more important than people and where the first rule is silence."[20] For Harry, imprisoned at first under the Dursleys' stairs and later forced to tell people that he is a student at St. Brutus' Secure Center for Criminally Incurable Boys, "reformatory" seems an apt metaphor. In Book 3, we read that "For years Aunt Petunia and Uncle Vernon had hoped that if they kept Harry as downtrodden as possible, they would be able to squash the magic out of him," and perhaps they think that all of this is for his own good.[21] It is certainly for theirs.

Families are our first community, but Harry, in time-honored literary fashion, is an orphan, cut off from loving parents and forced into the care of strangers, these Dursleys. Another notable orphan is Tom Riddle, whose upbringing at the orphanage we observe in Dumbledore's memories in *Half-Blood Prince* suggests that his emotional needs were quite as badly ignored as were Harry's. Throughout, Rowling draws parallels between the two, the Dark Lord and The Chosen One, yet one boy becomes a hero, the other a villain; one tries to reclaim family, one rejects it.

Harry is constantly filled with desire for communion with the family he lost. In his first adventure, when Harry discovers the Mirror of Erised and sees his mother and father within it, he becomes so taken with the images that he loses interest in all other activities—until Dumbledore discovers what he is doing. Dumbledore cautions Harry against the Mirror, for "It shows us nothing more or less than the deepest, most desperate desire of our hearts. You, who have never known your family, see them standing around you . . . It does not do to dwell on dreams and forget to live, remember that."[22] Dumbledore, who according to Rowling would have seen his own mangled family whole and alive in the Mirror (not, as he tells Harry, a warm pair of thick woolen socks), knows whereof he speaks.[23] Harry's desire for attachment to the parents he has never known can never be realized, and so could paralyze him in the present—or could it be realized? For Harry's family continues to pop up during his adventures. In *Prisoner of Azkaban*, he believes that he and Sirius have been saved from Dementors by his father's Petronus charm—although Harry later discovers that it was he himself, traveling back in time, who cast that spell. In *Half-Blood Prince*, Harry imagines that the marvelous potion-maker who had used his potions text before him was actually his father, although there is little real evidence of that.

Harry learns early that it is impossible for magic to truly raise the dead, but it must be difficult indeed not to seek communion with your family when you live in a world in which magic like the Mirror of Erised can dredge their memories up for you again, willingly or unwillingly. At the end of *Philosopher's Stone*, Hagrid gives Harry a photo album full of magically moving wizard pictures of his parents; in *Prisoner of Azkaban*, the foul magic of the Dementors forces Harry to relive the deaths of his parents when he was an infant, sounds that would otherwise have been unavailable to him; in various memories of Snape's and Dumbledore's, Harry witnesses his parents as children and Hogwarts students; in the collision of his wand with Voldemort's at the end of *Order of the Phoenix*, Harry's parents are brought back to a sort of life, as they are by

49

the Resurrection Stone shortly before Harry offers his own life in Book 7.

Forging Families—and Character

These are mere simulacra of family, however; for real relationship, Harry requires flesh and blood, and this is what he discovers at Hogwarts. As he and the other first years wait nervously to enter the hall, Professor McGonagall says, "Before you take your seats in the Great Hall, you will be sorted into your houses. The Sorting is a very important ceremony because, while you are here, your house will be something like your family within Hogwarts. You will have classes with the rest of your house, sleep in your house dormitory, and spend free time in your house common room."[24] The boy who has never been a part of a family before is now going to be launched into the midst of community.

Through his relationships with Hermione and Ron and in his time with the Weasleys (Harry's favorite family), who begin hosting Harry for portions of holidays starting in Book 2, Harry learns about the unqualified acceptance of family. When Harry goes to be with the Weasleys, what he finds most different from his time with the Dursleys is not the clanking of pipes from the ghoul or the random explosions from Fred and George's room; it is the strange and unaccountable "fact that everybody there seemed to like him."[25] They do more than like him, of course; Hermione and all of the Weasleys—even the ambitious Percy, who for several novels is on the outs with his family—will love, support, sacrifice for, and fight on Harry's behalf, and before the saga is complete, some will be badly wounded or even killed in the struggle against Voldemort.

Later in his education, Harry will meet his godfather, Sirius Black, another orphan who found a family at Hogwarts that shaped his life and gave it meaning, although their time together proves too brief. Harry grieves in *Half-Blood Prince*, since "the fact that he had had someone outside Hogwarts who cared what happened to him, almost like a parent, had been one of the best things about discovering his godfather. . . . and now the post owls would never bring him that comfort again."[26] Although someday Harry will form

50

his own family with Ginny Weasley and, it appears, give his children the stable and loving home he never had, in the present action of the novel Harry experiences little of real community through those to whom he is related; but since we are made to be in community, he seeks it elsewhere. His realization in Book 4 "that he would rather be here [at Hogwarts] and facing a dragon than back on Privet Drive with Dudley" marks the contrast between the two places.[27] One of them is a home in name only; the other has become Harry's home in fact.

For Harry, Hogwarts is indeed the community within which his moral formation takes place, an extended family with a father figure (Dumbledore), brother and sister (Ron and Hermione), spinster aunt (Professor McGonagall), and eccentric uncle (Hagrid), as well as the home he never expected to find. It also reveals some essential facts about community—those wildly diverse "family members" are actually a central part of his formation. Hogwarts exemplifies this regard for unity amidst difference from its very formation; the four founders of Hogwarts (Helga Hufflepuff, Rowena Ravenclaw, Godric Gryffindor, and Salazar Slytherin), different though they each were, believed that their differences could create a formative experience for the students of the larger school. As the Sorting Hat sings at the beginning of term in *Goblet of Fire,*

51

> They shared a wish, a hope, a dream,
> They hatched a daring plan
> To educate young sorcerers
> Thus Hogwarts School began.
> Now each of these four founders
> Formed their own house, for each
> Did value different virtues
> In the ones they had to teach.[28]

Rowling says that she designed the four houses at Hogwarts to conform to the four elements, all of which are necessary to form the universe (Hufflepuff, earth; Ravenclaw, air; Gryffindor, fire; Slytherin, water): "It was this idea of harmony and balance, that you had four necessary components and by integrating them you would make a very strong place."[29] Moreover, it would make for a strong and balanced community. Hogwarts is a vision of a body with many members in which not all have the same function. Rowling herself spoke of the need to have four different houses by saying, "You have to embrace all of a person, you have to take them with their flaws and everyone's got them. It's the same way with a student body. If only they could achieve perfect unity, you would have an absolutely unstoppable force, and I suppose it's that craving for unity and wholeness that means that they keep the quarter of the school that maybe does not encapsulate the most generous and noble qualities . . . in the very Dumbledore-esque hope that they will achieve union, and they will achieve harmony."[30]

The ideal community recognizes that not everyone shares the same function, yet all are essential to the operation of the whole. So it is that each house represents a cardinal virtue: Students sorted into Gryffindor tend to be courageous, Hufflepuffs hardworking, Slytherins ambitious, Ravenclaws intellectual. And even within houses there is diversity of gifts. Within Gryffindor, renowned for bravery, we nonetheless find diverse wizards: Harry is brilliant at defense against the dark arts; Neville is a gifted herbologist; Fred and George Weasley create complicated gag gifts; Pavarti Patil is drawn to divination; Hermione excels at transfiguration.

It is true that members of houses compete for things like the Quidditch team and dates to the Yule Ball and that the four houses are pitted against each other in formal competition, more "us" versus "them" differentiation. The House Cup is a primary plot element of the first three Potter novels, but it becomes clear as the stakes become higher in the later books that this competition is not nearly so important as it at first seemed. In fact, as the dangers mount and the challenges come hard and fast, what matters is people coming together to confront a common problem. At the conclusion of *Goblet of Fire*, Dumbledore addresses the assembled students—including those from the rival wizarding schools Durmstrang and Beauxbatons—about the necessity of their coming together to face difficult times: "The Triwizard Tournament's aim was to further and promote magical understanding. In the light of what has happened—of Lord Voldemort's return—such ties are more important than ever before. . . . we are only as strong as we are united, as weak as we are divided." Although Voldemort was uniquely skilled in creating discord and pushing people apart, Dumbledore said this did not have to be the case; wizards could fight the malice of He-Who-Must-Not-Be-Named "by showing an equally strong bond of friendship and trust."[31]

This trust between houses does seem to grow in the course of the books, so that when we reach the end of the story in Book 7, when Slytherin Pansy Parkinson suggests to the assembled houses in the Great Hall that they grab Harry and turn him over to Voldemort, the response from all but the Slytherins is immediate and unanimous: Gryffindors, Hufflepuffs, and Ravenclaws stand to their feet and draw their wands, forming a barrier between Harry and any who might hurt him, all of them united around their belief in him and in each other.[32]

This solidarity is not singular; by this time, Gryffindors, Hufflepuffs, and Ravenclaws have been united before, as we shall see, in the student organization known as Dumbledore's Army, formed in *The Order of the Phoenix*, and in the actual Order of the Phoenix as well. But what of the House of Slytherin? Are they, as Pansy's outburst and the house's subsequent slinking away from the forthcoming battle in *Deathly Hallows* suggest, simply outsiders, the "them" to be expelled, at best, and destroyed at worst? By no means. Professor Horace Slughorn, the Head of Slytherin, is roused to fight back against Voldemort and the Death Eaters in the final battle, and he himself duels the Dark Lord, alongside McGonagall and Kingsley Shacklebolt; Regulus Black, younger brother of Sirius, turns against the Dark Lord and steals one of Voldemort's Horcruxes at the cost of his own life; and Severus Snape spends his entire life watching over Harry, a child he loathes, to atone for the wrong he did as a young man in allowing Lily Potter to be killed. At the conclusion of Book 7, the old Slytherin headmaster, Phineas Nigellus Black, joins the portraits of all the former Hogwarts headmasters in applauding the victorious Harry, Ron, and Hermione, and he calls out, "And let it be noted that Slytherin House played its part! Let our contribution not be forgotten!"[33]

Rowling is clear that while the vast majority of dark wizards may emerge from Slytherin, the Noble House of Slytherin is also necessary for the health of the Hogwarts body. Our experience in these books is somewhat lopsided, she suggests, because it is almost entirely from the perspectives of Malfoy, Crabbe, and Goyle, Harry's nemeses. "You are seeing Slytherin house always from the perspectives of Death Eaters' children. They are a small fraction of the total Slytherin population. I'm not saying all the other Slytherins are adorable, but they're certainly not Draco."[34] Ambition, the cardinal virtue of Slytherins, can lead some to explore dark magic, but it is also a prerequisite for greatness, perhaps one of the reasons the Sorting Hat originally suggested that Harry might do well in Slytherin:

> "Not Slytherin, eh?" said the small voice. "Are you sure? You could be great, you know, it's all here in your head, and Slytherin will help you on the way to greatness, no doubt about that—no? Well, if you're sure—better be GRYFFINDOR!"[35]

Ambition unchecked can lead to danger, but in truth, the defining qualities of any of the houses could be a bad thing if overemphasized or left unchecked—too much book learning, or resolute hard work, or bravery would also unbalance a life and perhaps damage a person and those around him.

One must have, at the very least, tolerance if diverse people are going to live and work together, because this diversity is, as the founders of Hogwarts—and later Albus Dumbledore—knew, necessary for the development of the whole. The Slytherins may be difficult, but nonetheless, they are part of the community, a valuable part, to be forgiven as many times as necessary to keep them within the family. It may not be possible for members of this artificial family to be close; sometimes, as seems to be the case with the Malfoys, tolerance seems to be as far as anyone can possibly go. At the conclusion of the Battle of Hogwarts, when fifty of Harry's friends and followers lie dead, the Malfoys sit, unmolested, in the Great Hall of Hogwarts as mourning goes on around them; they are not welcomed with open arms, but in the general joy, as everywhere Harry looks he sees families reunited, they share that joy of reunion, and, perhaps, they begin to repent for the things they have done to those around them in the name of the Dark Lord they served so unwisely.[36]

Harry and his friends save Draco's life—twice!—in *Deathly Hallows*, yet in the final chapter, set nineteen years after the climactic Battle of Hogwarts, Draco's son Scorpius (like Harry's Albus Severus) is headed to his first year at Hogwarts, but Draco still stands apart from the other parents on Platform 9¾: "Draco caught sight of Harry, Ron, Hermione, and Ginny staring at him, nodded curtly, and turned away again."[37] Rowling, likewise, suggested in an interview that while Draco and Harry might have "a kind of rapprochement, in that Harry knows Draco hated being a Death Eater . . . [and] Draco would feel a grudging gratitude toward Harry for saving his life . . . Real friendship would be out of the question . . . Too much had happened prior to the final battle."[38] Perhaps Harry and Draco will never be friends. But still, there they both stand, two fathers, both seeing their beloved children off to Hogwarts.

Draco is gathered into the light, albeit somewhat unwillingly and tentatively; so too are some who are no longer with us, such as Severus Snape, one-time Head of Slytherin. When in the final chapter of the saga Harry's son Albus Severus tells his father that he fears the Sorting Hat will place him into Slytherin, Harry reminds him that he was named for two headmasters of Hogwarts, one of whom was a Slytherin. If the Sorting Hat puts him into Slytherin, "then Slytherin House will have gained an excellent student, won't it? It doesn't matter to us, Al."[39] The important thing about this sorting, as Harry has long known, is that choice enters into it. Who you are is less a matter of what someone else decrees about you and, as Dumbledore had told Harry at the end of *Chamber of Secrets*, more about what you choose. Similarly, Dumbledore tells Cornelius Fudge in *Goblet of Fire*, "it matters not what someone is born, but what they grow to be!"[40] Choice is an essential element in moral formation.

We cannot choose our families (although we can choose our relation to them), but in the communities Harry does choose there is much we can learn. During his time at Hogwarts, Harry chooses friendships, chooses to lead the student organization called

55

Dumbledore's Army, and chooses to affiliate himself with the anti-Voldemort group called the Order of the Phoenix. These choices reveal much about what we are called to be and do.

Members and Friends

With the help of Hermione and Ron, Harry is involved in the creation of a diverse group of students seeking to learn Defense Against the Dark Arts in contravention of Dolores Umbridge's teaching—and policies. They gather specifically in response to Harry's news about Voldemort's return: "I want to be properly trained in Defense [Against the Dark Arts] because," Hermione tells the assembled group, "Lord Voldemort's back."[41]

The students take the name "Dumbledore's Army" in response to Umbridge's ridiculous fears that if the students learn real magic they'll form a militia Dumbledore can lead against the Ministry of Magic. Under Harry's tutelage, they train assiduously for their real purpose—confronting dark magic. In their time together, this group forms attachments to each other and to the cause they fight for. They support each other, with Harry teaching them and the others reinforcing his teaching. They communicate with each other—Hermione enchants fake Galleons they can use as magical pagers. And they stand up for each other—in Umbridge's office, when Umbridge is about to torture Harry for information about who he has been communicating with, Hermione, obeyer of rules and respecter of authority, comes up with a devious plan to get her and Harry out of that office—a plan that ultimately gets Umbridge carried off by centaurs into the Forbidden Forest. Then when Harry heads to the Department of Mysteries thinking he is going to save Sirius, he is convinced to let Neville, Ginny, and Luna come along with him, Ron, and Hermione:

> "We were all in the D.A. together," said Neville quietly. "It was all supposed to be about fighting You-Know-Who, wasn't it? And this is the first chance we've had to do something real—or was that all a game or something?"
>
> "No—of course it wasn't—" said Harry impatiently.

"Then we should come too," said Neville simply. "We want to help."[42]

When Ginny, Neville, and Luna join Harry, Hermione, and Ron in invading the Ministry of Magic's Department of Mysteries to keep Voldemort from gaining the prophecy he seeks, the notion of community takes its most substantial shape and begins to show its function. This is, as Harry notes, not the group he would have put together; "he would not have picked Ginny, Neville, or Luna."[43] But they pull together, they fight together, and as Hauerwas said, they help each other become who they are supposed to be.

We have said that Harry is formed by others, but this same type of formation is true of many within the Hogwarts community. We can see radical change most clearly in the person of Neville Longbottom, son of members of the first Order of the Phoenix who were tortured into insanity; as Dumbledore later relates, both Harry and Neville were born at the right time to fulfill the prophecy that a child would destroy Voldemort, so Neville could just as easily have been Voldemort's target instead of Harry. During the first books, Neville seems to be a bumbling incompetent as unlikely to live up to his grandmother's grandiose hopes for him as he is to be the prophesied One who will defeat the Dark Lord. However, by the time Book 7 has ended, we can see that Neville has been transformed by his time among friends who support and encourage him. Neville becomes the focal point for anti-Voldemort activity at Hogwarts when Harry, Ron, and Hermione do not return to school for their final year, and he leads a guerilla war against new headmaster Severus Snape and the other Death Eaters on his faculty. Neville actually keeps hope alive at Hogwarts until Harry and the others arrive, and we can see how different he seems now compared to the boy who could do nothing right; thanks to his experiences with Harry, in the D.A., and in the Ministry, Neville has become a hero as well. When he welcomes Harry, Ron, and Hermione to the Room of Requirement toward the end of *Deathly Hallows*, he explains a little of what has gone on in their absence:

"Alecto, Amycus's sister, teaches Muggle Studies, which is compulsory for everyone. We've all got to listen to her explain how Muggles are like animals, stupid and dirty, and how they drove wizards into hiding by being vicious toward them . . . I got this one," he indicated another slash to his face, "for asking her how much Muggle blood she and her brother have got."

"Blimey, Neville," said Ron, "there's a time and a place for getting a smart mouth."

"You didn't hear her," said Neville. "You wouldn't have stood it either. The thing is, it helps when people stand up to them, it gives everyone hope. I used to notice that when you did it, Harry."[44]

In the end, Neville proves that Professor Trelawney's long-ago prophecy was valid, no matter which boy it referred to; while Harry's willing sacrifice is the most important element in the defeat of Lord Voldemort, it is Neville who produces the Sword of Gryffindor—which can only be drawn by a worthy Gryffindor—and slays the serpent Nagini. By the conclusion of the saga, Neville has grown into the man—and the wizard—he is supposed to be, the ultimate goal for any of us, and his friendships and membership in Dumbledore's Army are at the heart of his transformation.

This is likewise the way the organization known as the Order of the Phoenix functions: as a supportive community that forms around a set of beliefs and actions. During the First Wizarding War, this group assembles around Dumbledore and includes many younger wizards, including James and Lily Potter, Sirius Black, and Remus Lupin. The group re-forms when Voldemort returns at the end of *Goblet of Fire*, at the beginning of the Second Wizarding War.

Harry Potter meets all sorts of people: some who want to know him because he is famous, some who hate him because he is famous, some who look to him to be a leader, some who oppose him because of what he represents. But Harry is fortunate that in his life he finds a series of true friends who love and encourage him—and challenge him—to become the person he is meant to be. Among the most important of them is Dumbledore. Albus

Dumbledore was a friend to James and Lily Potter, a member with them in the first Order of the Phoenix, and it is Dumbledore we assume to have taken charge of details when the Potters were killed. He sets up Harry's stay with the Dursleys, and he seems to be responsible for the burial of the Potters and the setting up of their grave marker. And then, when Harry comes to Hogwarts, Dumbledore takes a special interest in him, looking after him, encouraging him, challenging him. Theirs is a relationship that marks Dumbledore as Harry's mentor and true friend.

We have observed that friendship is valuable and beautiful. But what, exactly, is a friend? The ancient world gave serious thought to this relationship. In Bronze Age epics, warriors are often depicted as brothers, their friendships sometimes closer even than sexual relationships. Xenophon, a student of Socrates, wrote a dialogue between his teacher and Critobulus on the topic of friendship. After discussing the sorts of self-serving and self-centered people one would not desire as a friend, Socrates turned to the question of whom to choose for true friendship: "I should say he must be just the converse of the above: he has control over the pleasures of the body, he is kindly disposed, upright in all his dealings, very zealous is he not to be outdone in kindness by his benefactors, if only his friends may derive some profit from his acquaintance."

When Critobulus asked how we might test those qualities before seeking friendship, Socrates answered, "How do we test the merits of a sculptor? Not by inferences drawn from the talk of the artist merely. No, we look to what he has already achieved. These former statues of his were nobly executed, and we trust he will do equally well with the rest." So a person who has been kind to his friends may be trusted, as Critobulus concludes from their discussion, to treat the newer friend as amiably.[45]

In these understandings, a true friend is a person whose works are unselfish, true, and beautiful, and whose earlier kindnesses to friends are well known. Dumbledore would certainly fit this description. Although Dumbledore seems to show up at important moments in Harry's life and always to be present at adventure's end to explain what has happened and what might happen next, it is not until *Order of the Phoenix* that we realize the degree to which Dumbledore has watched over Harry. At the end of *Order of the Phoenix*, he tells Harry how he has followed all that has happened to him over the years: "I defy anyone who has watched you as I have—and I have watched you more closely than you can have imagined—not to want to save you more pain than you had already suffered."[46] Surely this is what a friend does—watches, loves, tries to spare one from pain—but also calls a friend to her or his best self. As Rowling pointed out, "Dumbledore is a very wise man who knows that Harry is going to have to learn a few hard lessons to prepare him for what may be coming in his life. He allows Harry to get into what he wouldn't allow another pupil to do and he also unwillingly permits Harry to confront things he'd rather protect him from."[47]

In the Celtic tradition, people speak of the *anam cara*, the soul friend, and surely that is what Ron, Harry, and Hermione are to each other. Without an *anam cara*, we are lost, for we have no one with whom to share our truest selves, and it is here, of course, that Voldemort is most destitute. In response to an interview question about whether Voldemort had ever loved, Rowling responded, "No, he loved only power, and himself. He valued people whom he could use to advance his own objectives."[48] But nothing more. As Dumbledore told Harry after sharing with him his first memory of encountering the future Lord Voldemort, even as a boy, Tom Riddle did not want to be like anyone else or considered ordinary, and he certainly did not wish companions:

> I trust that you also noticed that Tom Riddle was already highly self-sufficient, secretive, and, apparently, friendless? . . . The adult Voldemort is the same. You will hear many of his Death Eaters claiming that they are in his confidence, that they alone are close to him, even understand him. They are deluded. Lord Voldemort has never had a friend, nor do I believe that he has ever wanted one.[49]

Many believe that they are Voldemort's *anam cara*; all are deluded, mere tools for him to use, and that is both their—and his—loss.

In this chapter we've explored the power of community in the Potter novels and in the world, and we'll close by considering the purposes of community. Like the new families formed in Harry Potter, like the communities coming together around a common mission, like the Order of the Phoenix, organizing as a force for justice and good, a true community gathers diverse people, begins the task of transforming them, and through them, begins to transform the world as well. The harmful values of society and the painful mistakes of individuals can begin to be corrected through this faithful, if imperfect, community—and it is to that act of transformation of a world gone dangerously wrong, to the heroic acts of sacrifice and good, that we turn now.

What is wrong with the world? How can we hope to fix it? What values will be life-giving, and how can we have the courage to champion them? Harry, Hermione, Ron, and their friends and family show us that we must learn to choose between what is right and what is easy, as well as how to recognize those things so that we can choose wisely.

61

3

Doing What Is Right

Heroism, Good, and Evil

"Remember, if the time should come when you have to choose between
what is right and what is easy, remember what happened to a boy who
was good, and kind, and brave, because he strayed across the path of
Lord Voldemort."

—Albus Dumbledore,
Harry Potter and the Goblet of Fire

"Clever as I am, I remain just as big a fool as anyone else."

—Albus Dumbledore,
The Tales of Beedle the Bard

Celebrity and Heroism

As I first write these words today in 2009, Western society is laying
to rest a famous person in a flurry of posthumous honor and uproar
(it happens to be Michael Jackson, although it might have been
any of a number of notables in the past one hundred years, from
Rudolph Valentino to Elvis to Princess Di to Anna Nicole Smith).
Hundreds of thousands flocked to pilgrimage sites connected with
the life, death, and remembering; traditional media covered the
death, aftermath, and mourning around the clock; blogs broke new

stories, memorial tweets took up over 30 percent of Twitter's capacity, and Facebook's memorial was its largest interactive event in history, with more participants than dropped in for the presidential inauguration of Barack Obama.[1] It was a firestorm of controversy and celebration and speculation—the sort of media event to which we have become accustomed, with one human life at its center.

Now, intending no disrespect, this cultural commotion was centered on the memory of a person who did not rescue people from a burning building, or throw himself on a live grenade to save his buddies, or cure cancer; while he displayed some admirable tendencies toward philanthropy and as a celebrity helped to bridge gaps between people of different races and cultures, this person was often controversial, and was best known for being well-known, for entertaining people, and while that may in fact be a valuable thing in and of itself, the tumult illustrates something about our culture.

We cannot differentiate between heroes and celebrities.

Harry Potter lives in such a world too, since it is also our world, with some magic tweaks of the imagination, and his life can teach us much about this question of heroism versus celebrity. As a baby, he becomes one of the most famous people in the Wizarding world, notable not for anything he has done himself, but for an accident of birth: born to a courageous set of parents who oppose Voldemort, who then sacrifice their lives for him when he is only an infant, Baby Harry becomes The Boy Who Lived, protected by the ancient magic of his mother's sacrificial death from Voldemort's Killing Curse. His survival, while noteworthy, could have happened to anyone, but since it happened to him, he is remembered and celebrated as the agent of the downfall of He-Who-Must-Not-Be-Named.

Like a prince, then, or like the scions of the rich and famous, Harry could have grown up gawked at and fussed over his whole life without having had to do anything to earn such approval. Dumbledore knows immediately that this sort of celebrity could stunt a person's moral and spiritual development, and so he gives Harry to his closest living relatives—the Dursleys—instead of permitting him to be raised in the Wizarding world. In response to Professor McGonagall's objection, "He'll be famous—a legend. . . . every child

in our world will know his name!" Dumbledore responds, "Exactly
. . . It would be enough to turn any boy's head. Famous before he
can walk and talk! Famous for something he won't even remember!
Can't you see how much better off he'll be, growing up away from
all that until he's ready to take it?"[2]

Celebrity doesn't leave Harry behind, even though he leaves the
Wizarding world for a decade; when he departs for his first year at
Hogwarts, he and his lightning-shaped scar are still famous. Inside
the Leaky Cauldron, Harry finds himself surrounded by people who
count themselves honored to meet him, and shaking hands with
everyone in the pub, and on the Hogwarts Express, Harry is an
object of interest and admiration. The reactions of Fred and George
Weasley—and Harry's matter-of-fact response to them—can summa-
rize this phenomenon for us:

> "Blimey," said the other twin. "Are you—?"
> "He is," said the first twin. "Aren't you?" he added to
> Harry.
> "What?" said Harry.
> "*Harry Potter*," chorused the twins.
> "Oh, him," said Harry. "I mean, yes, I am."[3]

Later in Harry's first year—after becoming a Quidditch hero, and
after helping to prevent Lord Voldemort from laying his hands on
the Philosopher's Stone—he will actually have done things worthy of
admiration, but at this point in his story, Harry is a celebrity simply
because of who he is, as ridiculous as that may seem.

Throughout the saga, Rowling pokes fun at celebrity culture
and at the way the media fuel celebrity in an incestuous cycle that
helps sell their own products. In Book 2, the new Defense Against
the Dark Arts teacher, author Gilderoy Lockhart, constantly gives
Harry directions (unwanted and absurd though they may be) about
how to manage his celebrity. During the running of the Triwizard
Tournament, Harry, while hardly the most accomplished of the
Champions, is the one with the most exploitable story and history, so tabloid journalist Rita Skeeter pulls him into a janitor's
closet for an interview. And later, in *Half-Blood Prince*, after Minister of Magic Cornelius Fudge finally sees Voldemort face to face

and everyone realizes Harry was telling the truth all along, Harry becomes the focus of something like Beatlemania:

> People stared shamelessly as he approached. They even pressed their faces against the windows of their compartments to get a look at him. He had expected an upswing in the amount of gaping and gawping he would have to endure this term after all the "Chosen One" rumors in the *Daily Prophet*, but he did not enjoy the sensation of standing in a very bright spotlight.[4]

At this point we might hope that some of this attention is in response to Harry's integrity and courage, although, as the spotlight metaphor suggests, the response still seems more like that of audience and star. Harry is regarded as a celebrity, as much as, perhaps, he is admired as a hero.

At the same time as the Wizarding media feeds the flames of public desire for faux information, it also pushes scandal and misinformation about good people (making them, in a sense, celebrity villains, another familiar group). When Dumbledore becomes a foe of Ministry of Magic policies, the *Daily Prophet* attacks him daily and mercilessly, and during Harry's fifth year, the *Prophet* makes Harry into a different kind of celebrity—a tabloid joke. His account of Voldemort's return is marked down to a desire on Harry's part to continue to be the sort of celebrity he never wanted to be in the first place, as Harry's friends have long known. When Draco Malfoy taunts Harry for being dragged into Gilderoy Lockhart's spotlight in *Chamber of Secrets*, for example, Ginny Weasley immediately steps in and defends Harry: "'Leave him alone, he didn't want all that!' said Ginny."[5] Although Ron will forget this in his jealousy over Harry's choice as Triwizard Champion, he comes to Harry after the first Triwizard trial and apologizes; the film version of *Goblet of Fire* makes this moment of recognition sharper and even funnier:

> Ron: I reckon you'd have to be barking mad to put your own name in the Goblet of Fire.

Harry may fantasize about winning the Triwizard Cup and how that might make him look to Cho Chang, but by the time the Tournament ends, he is more than happy to be done with it, and he works hard to give away his prize money. In any case, while Harry may enjoy a bit of adulation as much as the next teenage boy, his life and work prove that Dumbledore was right; by being raised outside of the spotlight, Harry has not developed an addiction to fame and glory that would lead him to pursue these dark gods over the light.

When we mistake celebrities for heroes (or seek to treat heroes as celebrities), we do so because celebrities have attained—or seem to have attained—the values our culture treasures most: wealth, power, and prominence. Harry, left a small fortune by his dead parents, is rich in Galleons, although he tends to spend frugally on everything but candy; his standoff with the Dark Lord in his infancy is attributed to personal power, as are his later near escapes; and, as Malfoy observes, putting Harry on the cover sells papers. He's one of the most famous people in the Wizarding world. People want to read about him, whether he is depicted as the poor little orphan missing his mother or as the juvenile delinquent who should be bounced out of Hogwarts, and that fame breeds media coverage.

Gilderoy Lockhart provides a sterling example of what happens when we confuse celebrity for heroism. Ever quick to seek the spotlight, to criticize the efforts of others, and to suggest that, if he were only given the chance, he could solve the problem of the Chamber of Secrets and the attacks on Hogwarts students, Lockhart is finally given that chance by the Hogwarts faculty, sick of listening to his hollow boasts. But when Harry and Ron go to his office to enlist his help to break into the Chamber of Secrets, rescue Ginny Weasley, and confront whatever dark secret they find there, they find that their teacher has a very different set of plans; his office has been stripped bare of all his possessions, and he clearly is packing for a quick getaway.

"What about my sister?' said Ron jerkily.

"Well, as to that—most unfortunate—" said Lockhart, avoiding their eyes as he wrenched open a drawer and started emptying the contents into a bag. "No one regrets more than I—"

"You're the Defense Against the Dark Arts teacher!" said Harry. "You can't go now! Not with all the Dark stuff going on here!"

67

"Well—I must say—when I took the job—" Lockhart muttered, now piling socks on top of his robes, "nothing in the job description—didn't expect—"

"You mean you're *running away?*" said Harry disbelievingly. "After all that stuff you did in your books—"

"Books can be misleading," said Lockhart delicately.[6]

Indeed they can; it emerges that Lockhart has not even been writing about his own adventures, but those of witches and warlocks whose memories he has then erased. His self-promotion, his best-selling books, all emerge from a false history; "Gilderoy Lockhart" is a creation completely of the media.

Harry differs from Lockhart and other celebrities of the Wizarding world (and of our own culture) in important ways. While Harry is, as Rowling notes, "flawed and mortal," and so is (like all of us) subject to desires and mistakes, his deepest values are not the values of his culture; in the ongoing struggle to choose between what is right and what is easy—or, in moral terms, between what is right and what is wrong—Harry consistently makes the right choices.[7]

68 He is a person who values community, having been alone, who is willing to sacrifice for others, having been saved through sacrifice himself, and who knows that the spotlight is a lonely and artificial place. While people may try to appropriate Harry—or may misunderstand him enough to think he wants glory—Rowling has created a very human, but very noble, person from whom we can learn much about heroism and sacrifice. This arises from the tropological level of reading, where great stories can impel us to do something; Harry's story tells how not to act, and suggests how we *should* act.

We've considered Harry's life in community, and shown how in contrast to many Western notions privileging individuality above all, Harry is at his best—and is his best—when surrounded by a loving and supportive community. While the glare of the Wizarding world's attention may always be on him, he is shy, unassuming, and does not realize his self-worth from how many column inches he gets in the *Daily Prophet*. He also learns to make friends based on the worth of the people he loves, not on what they possess or how popular they might be. Harry chooses from the beginning to value

substance over surface, rejecting Draco Malfoy's proffered friendship for the company of Hermione and Ron, and prompting this
response:

> [Draco] turned back to Harry. "You'll soon find out some wizard-
> ing families are much better than others, Potter. You don't want
> to go making friends with the wrong sort. I can help you there.
> . . . You hang around with riffraff like the Weasleys and that
> Hagrid, and it'll rub off on you."[8]

Harry, does, of course, continue to hang around with such riff-raff;
it becomes one of his finest and most defining qualities.

We can see that Harry is not interested in surfaces and superfici-
ality through Harry's long and real friendship with Ron and the Weasleys, who have much less of what the world values than the Malfoys.
The Weasleys are poor; Mr. Weasley is a mid-level bureaucrat—an
office drone, so to speak; Mrs. Weasley is described as dumpy and
unfashionable (by Draco Malfoy, admittedly, although perhaps no
one would describe Mrs. Weasley as fashionable). But none of those
superficial details matter; they are Harry's favorite family because
they accept him, love him, and love each other.

We can also see that Harry rejects superficial societal mores in
his other friendships. He befriends Hagrid, a half-giant, knowing
that inside that mammoth chest beats a loving and compassionate
heart. Professor Lupin, a werewolf, becomes a trusted confidant and
friend. And in his friendships with Luna and Neville, Harry clearly
is not seeking social approval. In *Half-Blood Prince*, when some of
his adoring fans invite him to travel with them, thinking perhaps
he is stuck with Neville and Luna, Harry quickly and thoroughly
disabuses them of the notion:

> "They're friends of mine," said Harry coldly.
> "Oh," said the girl, looking very surprised. "Oh. Okay." . . .
> "People expect you to have cooler friends than us," said
> Luna, once again displaying her knack for embarrassing honesty.
> "You are cool," said Harry shortly. "None of them was at the
> Ministry. They didn't fight with me."[9]

69

Perhaps friendship with those who have nothing material to add to one's bank account or reputation doesn't seem much like heroism compared to the other things Harry does in the course of his story, but it requires courage nonetheless, and it indicates a lot about the person willing to do it, especially when that person could fraternize with the rich and famous, dine out in high society simply on his fame. And yes, to love people who will bring society's condemnation on you—and to do so without expectation of anything in return—is heroic; note how rarely people do it in our culture, and I'm sure you'll agree. By the time Harry has reached his sixth year at Hogwarts, he has learned this lesson well, and Professor Horace Slughorn's attempts to collect him, as the professor has always gathered together the best, brightest, and most-connected students, have no allure for him. When it comes time to invite someone to Slughorn's Christmas party, the social event of the season, though many Hogwarts girls would leap at the chance to go with him, Harry invites his friend Luna, to Ron's dismay: "You could have taken *anyone!*" said Ron in disbelief over dinner. "*Anyone!* And you choose Loony Lovegood?"[10] Disapproval comes from more than just Ron; "an unusually large number of girls" wait in the entrance hall, staring resentfully at Harry when he meets Luna to go to the party.[11] But Harry appreciates qualities in Luna others don't, and he is delighted to escort her to her first big party.

Sacrifice is another countercultural value, and like friendship with those society looks down on, is in its own way as heroic as outwitting a dragon. Human beings are prone to want the most, the best, and the newest; they always want more. So it is that Dumbledore says of the Philosopher's Stone, the embodiment of this bad habit: "As much money and life as you could want! The two things most human beings would choose above all—the trouble is, humans do have a knack of choosing precisely those things that are worst for them."[12] Humans beings are innately selfish, and while our villain Voldemort is self-centered and acquisitive, he is not uniquely so. Western culture is driven by desire, by people making things, buying things, and selling things other people want. But Harry, while he too wants the best broomstick and would love to have some clothes not passed down from Dudley, has sacrifice in his genes; his father and mother give their lives in hopes of saving him, and this resonates in his thoughts and actions. As Rowling said, Harry saves people; it's what he does, often without thought for the consequences to himself. When a person is able to put his own needs aside and concentrate on the good of others—and the good of the world—he or she has reached the core of heroism.

Perhaps the greatest acknowledged expert on the hero is Joseph Campbell, who studied cultural and literary hero myths all over the world to construct what we now know as the archetypal Hero's Journey. Campbell noted, first, that "The hero is the man of self-achieved submission. But submission to what?"[13] Campbell's study showed that this "what" was submission of his or her own desires to the greatest needs of others, with truly mythic heroes helping to achieve something like a new society—or even a new creation. A mythic hero returned from his adventures bearing "the means for the regeneration of his society as a whole," not simply bearing the spoils of victory for himself.[14] Elsewhere, Campbell boiled down heroism in this way, again emphasizing self-sacrifice and the common good: "The hero is the one who comes to participate in life courageously and decently . . . not in the way of personal rancor, disappointment, or revenge."[15] So, self-sacrifice, courage, decency— and a new world, of sorts, that emerges from the hero's actions; we find all of these in Harry's life and work, and so in a classical sense, we can say that Harry is the purest and truest of heroes—someone who risks himself and all he has on behalf of others—and whose sacrifice makes a difference in the world.

Knowing Evil

Rowling sets up a contrast that seems to be important between her most heroic characters—the Potters, Dumbledore, and Harry himself—and her great villain, Lord Voldemort, when it comes to the question of death. The heroes seem willing to give their lives; the villain clings to it, doing whatever evil is necessary to keep it. Death is a universal fact, although that fact can take on so much importance that clearly it can choke out more important matters. An obsessive fear of death—or an obsessive hope that a heaven lies after this life—can badly misshape our earthly lives, which would be (and is) tragic. We can observe the negative effects in Lord Voldemort, or we can listen to the wisdom of Dumbledore, who also suggests that this obsessive notice of death is misplaced; in *Sorcerer's Stone*, Dumbledore tells Harry that "to the well-organized mind, death is but the next great adventure," and this demystifying of death is a motif throughout the story.[16]

Dumbledore, of course, goes on to practice what he preaches. In his refusal to let death control him, Dumbledore echoes the sentiments of great philosophers throughout history who thought of death not as something to be feared by those in the right state of reflection or spirit, but as something that shapes us into who we are meant to become if we acknowledge it. Socrates said that the true philosopher was the person who was ready to die; Seneca said that a person will live badly who does not know how to die well; Heidegger observed that the reality of death gives people the existential nudge that forces people to become themselves. All these philosophers agree that learning to accept death is an important part of understanding oneself and one's place in the cosmos—and it may be impossible for us to know what matters, what is good and what is not, until we have.

While the good triumphs in the Harry Potter stories, as we had always hoped (and always hope), there can be no question that J. K. Rowling also recognizes the power and allure of evil. In Harry's story, evil proves to be a reality of human life, tempting even good characters to do things they should not, and we can see through the lives of evil characters how weakness, cruelty, and venality can enter into and totally misshape a human life. Every great adventure story needs a great villain—a Professor Moriarty, a Dracula, a Hannibal Lecter, a Darth Vader—and we are fortunate as readers of the Potter novels to have one of the greatest, Voldemort. Voldemort and those like him can teach us much about how evil works, where evil comes from, and how we can recognize evil even in places where we don't normally look. Because of this, He-Who-Must-Not-Be-Named should be named as our benefactor.

Evil shows its face in many ways in the Potter saga. It can be banal, such as Gilderoy Lockhart's, a greed for money and fame that marks him simply as one who chooses the gods of our society; it can be opportunistic, such as Lucius Malfoy's, who is inclined toward evil but only pursues it when he knows it will be rewarded, not punished; it can be cowardly, such as Peter Pettigrew's craven disguise as a rat to avoid punishment, and his return to Voldemort only because he has nowhere else to go; it can be sadistic, such as Bellatrix Lestrange's delight in causing pain. But at the heart of the book's depiction of evil is the Dark Lord, Voldemort, who epitomizes everything Harry struggles against—and so we will turn to him and his followers to help us explore evil—from a reader's standpoint, of course—in all of its various forms.

The contrast between Harry's heroic qualities of compassion, sacrifice, and bravery with Voldemort is sharp; Voldemort, who sets himself apart, who is truly known by no one, who will sacrifice anyone and anything to his plans, is the embodiment of evil in the Potter novels, but it is important to understand what Rowling regards evil to be and how it may help enlighten us. Too often we can glibly regard others as evil and ourselves as good, and Rowling's world complicates matters a bit. Can one, for example, perform an evil act with the intention of doing ultimate good? Can a person hold evil thoughts—or perform evil acts—and then repent of them? Can groups and institutions be guilty of evil as well as individuals? Harry's story suggests many real-world connections that force us to think long and hard about the problem of evil in our own lives, not just in those we would label villains.

Let's consider first what Rowling's own understanding of evil might be. She has often said that she considers prejudice to be a great evil that many people knowingly or unconsciously practice, and she portrays how terrorism and violence deaden the souls of those who commit it and those who must endure it. In her depiction of Voldemort as a person who callously takes life, she suggests that murder is an ultimate evil. Clearly, Rowling recognizes the reality of evil and depicts it honestly as a fact of life. However, this tangible evil stands in sharp contrast to the self-sacrifice, nobility, and compassion exhibited by many other characters throughout the saga. It is clearly a sign that Rowling believes good is not only more beautiful, but ultimately more powerful than evil. Despite the atrocities of centuries—and centuries of belief in human depravity—Rowling, like a certain beloved Hogwarts headmaster, seems to want to see the good in people.

"Trusts people, he does. Gives them second chances," Hagrid says of Dumbledore in *Goblet of Fire* in the midst of a media landslide condemning Dumbledore's extension of teaching posts to werewolves and "part-humans" like Hagrid, "Dumbledore's Giant Mistake."[17] And truly, Dumbledore does hold out hope for fallen and damaged people—as well as for those who have simply made mistakes of judgment. Dumbledore prefers to judge people by their best impulses, rather than to condemn them for their worst. It's not that evil characters don't sometimes disappoint Dumbledore—Tom Riddle certainly proves to be an exception to Dumbledore's belief that humans beings are worthy of trust and that none are irredeemable—but it is significant, I think, that the wisest of characters in the Potter novels seems to believe in the inherent goodness and trustworthiness of people, the potential for almost all to be redeemed in the end.

None of this is to suggest that human evil does not exist; Rowling is neither a hopeless romantic nor blind to the realities of human existence. Mistakes and moral failures may be found even in the actions of our most admirable characters. Dumbledore gives in to an overwhelming urge to cheat death and bring back his sister; Harry attempts Unforgiveable Curses when enraged; Ron Weasley pleads to be turned loose to kill Death Eaters after Fred is murdered; Hermione attacks Ron with conjured birds in a fit of jealousy. Evil is a reality in Rowling's world and ours, and when it is indulged in, we witness what Paul Tillich refers to as "the state of estrangement" that emerges from our selfish choices and self-gratification. Evil is "diabolical" in the sense that it becomes an adversary to our best selves; it creates a chasm between ourselves and everything that should matter to us most.[18]

Dumbledore is ever talking about the necessity of choice, and moral choice is at the heart of Rowling's tale, although even the best characters can choose badly. However, human evil has a larger dimension than simply personal choice. In a useful formulation, Hendrikus Berkhof argued that evil can be manifested in three ways: in our own personal failings, through unhealthy interpersonal interactions, and in external relations, including our voluntary participation in corrupted institutions or our conscious or unconscious acceptance of cultural understandings by which we are shaped.[19]

In the realm of individual evil, we recognize that characters like Voldemort, Grindelwald, and Karkaroff give us clear examples of individual lives lived in opposition to all that matters, lives demonstrating the wrong choices that Dumbledore spoke about and the estrangements that Tillich described. In recognizing that evil characters exist in Harry Potter—and that good people sometimes do evil things—we see the power of personal evil and become attuned to the importance of finding a moral center that allows us to resist self-serving choices. But before we assess the understandings of evil that revolve around human choice and human agency, we should first examine—and eliminate—another traditional understanding of evil and its sources. The Dark Lord might seem, at first glance, to represent a superhuman and supernatural force of evil, similar perhaps to Sauron, Tolkien's Dark Lord in the world of *The Hobbit* and *The Lord of the Rings*. Voldemort certainly wants people to regard him as an elemental force of evil. He claims that he is no longer human, and he no longer appears to be human, but his fears and ambitions seem very human indeed. The primary difference between He-Who-Must-Not-Be-Named and other characters in the Potter novels is not that one is a supernatural being and the others are mortal; Voldemort is, as we all discover in *Deathly Hallows*, completely mortal. What sets him apart is that his fear of death has warped his soul to the extent that, using his great personal power, he chooses to perform horrible acts. This does not make him a cosmic force for evil, however much he might aspire to be, although he does share some of the characteristics associated with supernatural evil.

Like the various tempters of myth and story, Voldemort is able to induce people to do things they would not otherwise do—or perhaps, would not even conceive. In the First Wizarding War, we know that Voldemort and the Death Eaters employed the Imperius Curse to force many wizards to do their bidding, and we witness this form of domination again in the Second Wizarding War. Using the Imperius Curse on Pius Thicknesse, the Death Eaters gain the access to the Ministry that will ultimately lead to the death of Rufus Scrimgeour and the overthrow of the Ministry of Magic. As in the refrain, "The Devil made me do it," however, after the First War many reformed Death Eaters joined the Imperiused to claim that Voldemort and his followers forced them to do evil against their wills and consciences, and one wonders if perhaps there was a rush to claim this sort of magical insanity defense again after the Battle of Hogwarts. The fallout of the First War is confusion; as "Mad-Eye Moody" notes in his classroom lecture on the Unforgiveable Curses, these confessions left "Some job for the Ministry, trying to sort out who was being forced to act, and who was acting of their own free will."[20] In any case, we can see that the Dark Lord sows evil and discord in his wake, like many mythic gods of evil or as in certain understandings of the Devil.

Still, while Voldemort takes on many supernatural trappings, his very human fear of death still remains the most important reminder that he is merely a powerful—but human—villain. Unlike such characters as Sauron, Lord of Mordor, Voldemort is not a supernatural force, although he is certainly a frightening human face of evil, and his individual choices are a startling example of the ways a human being can damage his soul by elevating himself at the expense of all other things. Through the characters of He-Who-Must-Not-Be-Named, Barty Crouch Jr., Bellatrix Lestrange, and other such villains, we observe many individual choices to torture, overpower, maim, and kill, the ultimate destructive projections of power. We also witness other forms of evil, not all of them associated with characters we would consider evil—greed, selfishness, lust, gluttony. Even the personal vanity of Professor Slughorn, who for much of Harry's sixth year would rather preserve his reputation than give

Harry the memory he needs to fight Voldemort, represents evil; those of us who count ourselves good because we don't rob banks, mug the elderly, or take candy from babies must still acknowledge that when it comes to personal evil, small acts of commission—or omission—also matter.

But in addition to these examples of personal evil, characters also help us to understand interpersonal evil—the emergence or growth of evil as a result of relationships. For example, although Malfoy, Crabbe, and Goyle individually are not very pleasant, these three are worse when put together; they are more—or less—than the sum of their parts. More than any other clique to be found in Hogwarts School, these three are intimidating, violent, and generally unpleasant, and never more so than when Malfoy's brains directs the brawn of the others. We see their potential for mass evil most clearly in *Order of the Phoenix*, when they and other Slytherins are banded together to form Dolores Umbridge's Inquisitorial Squad, and their hatred of Harry, Ron, and Hermione is allowed free reign. Likewise, the Death Eaters, Voldemort's followers, are personally evil; Bellatrix Lestrange would be a horror even without a magic wand and an infatuation for the greatest dark wizard of all time. But membership in a community committed to darkness reinforces each individual Death Eater's darkness, just as we have discovered that a community of the good can lead to moral formation. Bellatrix is at her least lovely and most deadly when she is a Death Eater.

The historical record shows that humans have often been less moral in groups than they might have been individually, egged on or encouraged in their immoral acts by the presence of others—or by the actions of others (as the title of Reinhold Niebuhr's book *Moral Man and Immoral Society* suggests)—and the Death Eaters certainly exhibit this truth. While many of the Death Eaters were free in the decade Voldemort was gone to continue to perpetrate great evils, with few exceptions, they laid low; their evil actions were private and low-key. Individually, they were afraid to continue the intimidation, torture, and murder they had gloried in when they had been part of a group led by Voldemort. When Voldemort returns and the group re-forms, however, note how quickly they take courage and comfort. Witness the Death Eaters at the Quidditch World Cup, clad in robes and masks, secure in the darkness and their numbers; it's an intimidating if somewhat pathetic display directed at defenseless Muggles, and it would never have happened without community.

After Voldemort's return, we begin to see, for the second time, mass Muggle killings, Wizard death squads, intimidation, and control. Certainly the Dark Lord's presence and power inspire the Death Eaters to this visibility, these vile acts, but many of the evils perpetrated by the group could have been committed by the same individuals had they simply felt capable of them alone. They were not, which confirms for us that people feel safer to commit their evil with the support of their leader and other like-minded individuals alongside them. The Death Eaters resemble other elite groups in history who reinforce each other in evil and provide support, perhaps most obviously the Nazi SS, who as a group committed inhumanities that individuals have said that they might have been afraid to even contemplate.

78   Perhaps the most alarming aspect of the Potter books' treatment of evil, however, has to do not with what evil people choose to do, whether individually or in groups, but with social or institutional evil that continues because the alternative seems worse or more frightening and sometimes persists because people are ignorant—or uncaring—about injustices present in the system. People tend to limit their conception of sin and evil to that done by individuals, often expressing it in a set of moral condemnation for individual acts, but history—including, as Rowling understands, recent history—demonstrates that systems, since they are made up of sinful individuals, can also be purveyors of evil. In obvious references to the Blair and Bush governments' tolerance and even encouragement of actions like torture, rendition, and the politics of personal destruction, Rowling's epic shows Ministry of Magic officials committing evil acts to prop up the system they serve. Although these acts are carried out in the service of good and even noble causes, the judgment rings out clear in the Potter universe. "I don't like

your methods," is Harry's message for the Minister of Magic after he has been tortured by its representative, and there are ample reasons to second Harry's conclusion—and to employ it ourselves. When people begin to stand in the darkness in order to—they believe—safeguard the light, then gray is the inevitable result. Examples of this dangerous moral ambiguity abound in the Potter novels. For example, before we even enter the story, the Ministry of Magic—despite Dumbledore's sound reservations—has chosen to employ Dementors, foul, dark, and hideous creatures, as prison guards at Azkaban. J. K. Rowling has said that the use of Dementors is an early indication of the "underlying corruption of the Ministry."[21] These dark creatures inspire misery and fear, have the magical power to make a person relive his or her most horrible memories, and their kiss steals a person's soul—perhaps the most horrible act one can imagine. Still, fear leads us all to make strange alliances; when Dumbledore tells the Minister of Magic that the first step to prevent Lord Voldemort's rise to power is to remove Azkaban from the Dementors' control, Cornelius Fudge defends the policy:

79

> "Preposterous!" shouted Fudge again. "Remove the dementors? I'd be kicked out of office for suggesting it. Half of us only feel safe in our beds at night because we know the dementors are standing guard at Azkaban!"
>
> "The rest of us sleep less soundly in our beds, Cornelius, knowing that you have put Lord Voldemort's most dangerous supporters in the care of creatures who will join him the instant he asks them!" said Dumbledore.[22]

And Dumbledore is right of course, for the Dementors do eventually turn to You-Know-Who, and Fudge is forced to admit this defection to the Muggle Prime Minister:

> "I thought the dementors guard the prisoners at Azkaban," [the Prime Minister] said cautiously.
>
> "They did," said Fudge wearily. "But not anymore. They've deserted the prison and joined He-Who-Must-Not-Be-Named. I won't pretend that wasn't a blow."[23]

While they are still under Ministry control, however, Dolores Umbridge sends Dementors after Harry at the opening of Order of the Phoenix to try and discredit him—and if he had not successfully defended himself and Dudley, she would have been responsible for two deaths, or worse. These foul creatures attack the two schoolboys and try to suck their souls, and only Harry's skillful—and unauthorized—use of the Patronus Charm saves them.

Umbridge's decision to send a Dementor hit squad is a reprehensible action from anyone, let alone a high-ranking government official, and her willingness to risk the death or destruction of innocents in defense of an institution tells us much about the idea of institutional evil. But then again, Umbridge, who later in *Order of the Phoenix* is placed as the Ministry's official representative within Hogwarts, takes it upon herself to do many unpleasant things in her appearances in the books; she issues edicts limiting freedoms, judges the capabilities and loyalties of her fellow teachers, and, when she uncovers supposed disciplinary problems at Hogwarts, tortures her students. When Harry arrives to do his first detention with her—earned for telling the truth about Dumbledore's return—she seats him and tells him he will be writing *I must not tell lies* with her special quill—and as he writes, Harry finds those words sliced into the back of his own hand as the red ink flows onto the paper:

> Again and again Harry wrote the words on the parchment in what he soon came to realize was not ink, but his own blood. And again and again the words were cut into the back of his hand, healed, and then reappeared the next time he set quill to parchment.
>
> Darkness fell outside Umbridge's window. Harry did not ask when he would be allowed to stop. . . .
>
> "Come here," she said, after what seemed like hours.
>
> He stood up. His hand was stinging painfully. When he looked down at it he saw that the cut had healed, but that the skin there was red raw.[24]

This torture is not the least Dolores Umbridge is prepared to do to maintain the Ministry. Toward the end of *Order of the Phoenix*, her fear will lead her to even go so far as to endanger Harry's sanity

by casting an Unforgiveable Curse on him when he won't give her
the answers she believes she needs:

> "This is more than a matter of school discipline. . . . This is an
> issue of Ministry security. . . . You are forcing me, Potter. . . .
> I do not want to," said Umbridge, still moving restlessly on the
> spot, "but sometimes circumstances justify the use. . . . I am
> sure the Minister will understand that I had no choice . . . . The
> Cruciatus Curse should loosen your tongue." [25]

When Hermione tells Umbridge that the Minster of Magic would
not want her violating the law, Umbridge simply says that Fudge
will not have to know and thus will have no responsibility to act, a
classic example of plausible deniability.

Later, in *Deathly Hallows*, we see Umbridge operating a Star
Chamber, sitting in judgment over Muggle-born witches and wizards
that the Ministry—now under Voldemort's control—has decided to
eliminate, and as she does so, she is again surrounded by Dementors
who do her bidding, bringing the accused in and out, and prepared
to enforce discipline if anyone rebels.

Umbridge and other uncritical officials employ these techniques
because they believe them necessary to preserve order and maintain
power; as the world grows more terrifying, they seem, to some, to
be necessary measures. J. K. Rowling, who once worked for Amnesty
International, which records, protests, and tries to prevent torture
and political oppression around the world, is passionately opposed
to the notion that such practices could ever be defensible. As readers of these books knew, torture has been an element of the actual
war on terror, and during the writing and publication of the final
volumes of Harry Potter, news reports and photos indicated that
suspects and prisoners of war in such places as the Abu Ghraib
prison—once dictator Saddam Hussein's dungeon—had been tortured by Allied forces or delivered into the hands of friendly nations
with fewer legal restrictions against mistreatment of prisoners and
lower standards of human rights than those of Great Britain and the
United States.

These decisions were made by some who considered themselves
patriotic, loyal, and certain that their "difficult decisions" would

81

help save British and American lives by preventing future acts of terror; American Vice President Dick Cheney argued early on that to protect Americans from terrorism, it might be necessary to go to the "Dark Side." Some experts argue that torture and "enhanced interrogation" save lives, especially when they lead to actionable intelligence; others assert that they are ineffective, that they will lead instead only to whatever admissions the questioners desire. But both these pragmatic arguments beg the moral question: *Is torture right?* The question, we note, is not *Is torture legal?*, for in virtually every nation-state—including, of course, Britain and America—and in international law including the Geneva Conventions, it remains illegal. Redefining acts like waterboarding, temperature extremes, and sensory deprivation that had traditionally been considered torture as "enhanced interrogation" should not fool people any more than Umbridge's rationalizations; inflicting severe pain or distress on anyone as a punishment or to force them to act or talk is a textbook definition of torture, and thus the core question remains. Is torture an acceptable practice in times of anxiety and threat?

82

Rowan Williams, who as Archbishop of Canterbury also serves in the British House of Lords, says that any arguments about efficacy are irrelevant; we must "hold firm [to] the idea that torture is always and in every circumstance an inadmissible invasion of the dignity of the human person," and British journalist Peter Oborne wrote in the early stages of a breaking story on his nation's collusion with torture, "one of the most important distinguishing marks of a civilised society is the refusal to countenance torture."[26] Rowling would agree. When the Ministry of Magic, or its representatives, commits these evil acts in response to a perceived outside evil, it is lowering itself to the level of the Death Eaters themselves. As Williams noted about the forceful responses to the 9/11 attacks, state-sponsored acts may represent "legal violence," but the distinctions between what the "Enemy" has done and what may be done in an attempt to defend against the Enemy may become increasingly muddy, and the cost of this defense may become too high, since what we set out to defend has become corrupted in the process.[27]

We can lose what matters most to us when we become like those we hate or fear—to appropriate a familiar rhetoric from early in the war on terror, we might say that when we behave like the terrorists, the terrorists win, even if what we've done is now deemed to be "legal."

The system has the ability to manipulate the legal system, of course, to decide what is right and what is wrong. In *Deathly Hallows*, for example, Rufus Scrimgeour takes a law intended to prevent wizards from passing on dark magical artifacts and employs it to scrutinize the bequests in Albus Dumbledore's will:

> "You had no right to do that!" [Hermione] said, and her voice trembled slightly.
>
> "I had every right," said Scrimgeour dismissively. "The Decree for Justifiable Confiscation gives the Ministry the power to confiscate the contents of a will—"
>
> "That law was created to stop wizards passing on Dark artifacts," said Hermione . . . "Are you telling me that you thought Dumbledore was trying to pass us something cursed?"[28]

Because the Ministry makes laws—and administers them—it can twist the law as it wishes, and justice can be whatever the Ministry decides it is. Although it is an unjust decision, the Ministry passes a death sentence in *Prisoner of Azkaban* on the hippogriff Buckbeak, who attacked Draco Malfoy after being treated with contempt by the boy. Likewise the Minister of Magic refuses to listen to Harry and Hermione's evidence that it was Peter Pettigrew, not Sirius Black, who had been Voldemort's murderous servant, and he plans to have the Dementors administer their kiss, the equivalent of another death penalty:

83

> "Without Peter Pettigrew [said Dumbledore] . . . we have no chance of overturning Sirius's sentence."
>
> "*But you believe us.*"
>
> "Yes, I do," said Dumbledore quietly. "But I have no power to make other men see the truth, or to overrule the Minister of Magic."[29]

Later, after Voldemort has surreptitiously taken over the Ministry, repressive and unjust laws and policies are passed, and people like Dolores Umbridge carry them out, not knowing that their personal evil is actually in service of the even greater evil of a fallen system. Is it ironic or tragic that Umbridge never seems to notice the change at the top of the Ministry or that she performs similar actions under Cornelius Fudge and under Lord Voldemort's stooge, Pius Thicknesse? Both, perhaps.

Sometimes evil acts are perceived to be a function of maintaining a system (or are not defined or perceived as evil, since the system gets to define such things). However, sometimes maintaining a status quo does not require overt acts, but simply the quiet acquiescence of those who constitute an institution or society. Dolores Umbridge is actively serving Voldemort's purposes in the Ministry in *Deathly Hallows*, but so are the technicians, bureaucrats, and all those who continue to work within—or to blindly trust—the Ministry. Real-world examples of this inaction abound; in America during the civil rights era, for example, failing to question racial realities might not have been an act of conscious evil, but nonetheless, it allowed an unjust system to survive unhindered. Peter Gomes observes that American racism was served not only by the collective acts of violence by the Ku Klux Klan (America's own Death Eaters) and lynch mobs, but by "the system that encouraged and supported a culture of violence and discrimination. Individuals might repent and change their ways, but no real change would happen until the systems themselves were changed."[30]

While individual and interpersonal sin are real and damaging, and counted in most calls for morality, we cannot escape the reality of systemic evil, even if we would prefer to ignore it, because we are part of so many systems. It becomes, actually, an act of personal evil if we avert our eyes or prefer not to know. Rowling dramatically condemns unquestioning acceptance of "the way things are" such as the Wizarding world's denigration of magical creatures, in its denial of wands to all nonhumans, and, particularly, in the enslavement of house elves. While Hermione's campaign for house elves is sometimes treated as comic relief, it nonetheless represents an authentic issue of justice: as Rowling has said, the issue is that of slavery. Hermione recognizes this clearly: "'You do realize that your sheets are changed, your fires lit, your classrooms cleaned, and your food cooked by a group of magical creatures who are unpaid and enslaved?'"[31] Slavery is an evil we like to imagine as mostly dead, although sex workers and chocolate pickers are among the contemporary examples of people in slavery today.

The otherwise estimable *Hogwarts, A History*, to Hermione's great distress, does not include house elves, let alone their role behind the scenes at the school: "Not once, in over a thousand pages, does *Hogwarts, A History* mention that we are all colluding in the oppression of a hundred slaves!"[32] And except for Hermione and a few gentle-minded people such as Mr. Weasley and Dumbledore, few in the Potter saga even consider the feelings of house elves—they are, literally, out of sight and out of mind.

Rowling spoke of this human tendency to unknowingly participate in systemic evil in her speech to the Harvard graduates:

> And many prefer not to exercise their imaginations at all. They choose to remain comfortably within the bounds of their own experience. . . . They can refuse to hear screams or to peer inside cages; they can close their minds and hearts to any suffering that does not touch them personally; they can even refuse to know.
>
> But as she told the assembled graduates, this failure of imagination and curiosity is inexcusable, for it enables evil to continue: "without ever committing an act of outright evil ourselves, we collude with it, through our own apathy."[33]

It's just as Hermione says to Ron when he maintains, as Fred and George do, that house elves are happy in their role and therefore no action is necessary: "'It's people like *you*, Ron,' Hermione began hotly, 'who prop up rotten and unjust systems just because they're too lazy to—'"[34]

Or too apathetic, we might say.

"Constant vigilance" is Mad-Eye Moody's cry for wizards to be on the lookout for dark magic—but it might also be our watchword as we consider the many ways that evil and injustice can take root. When even the systems and institutions we are part of may be agents of injustice in the world, it's clear that constant vigilance is not just recommended, but vital.

Turning toward the Light

It is in recognizing our own evil—or our own collusion with sinful systems—that our movement toward wholeness can begin. In wisdom traditions, as in Harry Potter, we are enjoined to turn away from evil and toward good, to do what is right instead of what is easy—in a word that is often used and often misunderstood, to "repent." This word "repent" comes from the Greek word *metanoia*, and it refers not just to this turning way from evil, as repent suggests, but to a complete and deep-seated change in a person's life, a 180 degree turn away from evil and toward good. Rowling depicts *metanoia* over and over again, particularly in *Deathly Hallows*; in fact it might be said that the great theme of Book 7 is that of repentance and rebirth. The importance of remorse is expressed early on, when Hermione reveals that her research into Horcruxes reveals only one way to regain wholeness: "'Remorse,' said Hermione. 'You've got to really feel what you've done.'"[35] One must, in other words, repent one's past behavior, experience it as a wrong to be regretted and turned away from. Only then can one turn toward wholeness, begin to mend the state of estrangement in which one has placed oneself. It is a recipe for *metanoia*—repentance leading to a new and renewed state of being.

Indeed, *Deathly Hallows* might be called a catalog of *metanoia*, a series-concluding book in which almost every major character is presented with a chance to repent of his or her past evils and to mend. Some of these opportunities lead to changes that are unaccountable and nothing short of miraculous. Dudley Dursley, for example, has bullied Harry through a decade and a half of life, has never defended him, has never objected to the rank injustices visited on him. As we saw, Rowling presents Dudley as the Muggle counterpart to Draco Malfoy, who she describes as Harry's enemy "since their first journey to Hogwarts."[36] But when Harry saves Dudley from the Dementors at the beginning of *Half-Blood Prince*, it begins a process of remorse and redemption that climaxes when Dudley and his parents are being taken to safety at the beginning of *Deathly Hallows*. First, Dudley is the one who stands up against his father and says, loudly, "I'm going with these Order people."[37]

Then, when it becomes apparent to Dudley that Harry will not be going with them, he begins to manifest—incredibly—concern. He asks, "Why isn't he coming with us?" does not seem reassured by the explanations for why Harry won't accompany them, and when Harry tries to explain to his offended fellow Wizards why the Dursleys don't seem to care about him—"They think I'm a waste of space, actually"—Dudley objects.

> "I don't think you're a waste of space."
> If Harry had not seen Dudley's lips move, he might not have believed it. As it was, he stared at Dudley for several seconds. . . .
> "Well . . . er . . . thanks, Dudley."
> Again Dudley appeared to grapple with thoughts too unwieldy for expression before mumbling, "You saved my life."[38]

Harry begins to realize that Dudley has actually begun reaching out to him in small ways—like the cup of tea outside his door he'd stepped into that morning, cursing—although he is again stunned when Dudley crosses the room to shake his hand before departing:

> "Blimey, Dudley . . . did the dementors blow a different personality into you?"
> "Dunno," muttered Dudley. "See you, Harry."
> "Yeah . . . " said Harry, taking Dudley's hand and shaking it. "Maybe. Take care, Big D."[39]

Where there had been selfishness, violence, and unconcern, we now find something else. We also see the possibility of reconciliation between two boys who should have been brothers—and might still be, as a result of this transformation.

The power of the Dementors to make a person relive his worst memories seems to have been key; Rowling said that "when Dudley is attacked by the Dementors he saw himself, for the first time, as he really was. This was an extremely painful, but ultimately salutory lesson and began the transformation in him."[40] Remorse may be extremely painful, but it is also the path to a better life. To renounce evil, to turn toward good, requires that we regret the pain we have caused others, and Dudley's case is a powerful early example of how the action of *Deathly Hallows* focuses on reformation and transformation.

In small and great turns, characters express their remorse, admit their faults, and launch themselves into more abundant, more compassionate lives—or at least into some greater sympathy for them after their deaths. Sometimes these characters have been villains, like Dudley, or Severus Snape, or Percy Weasley, the first-officious and then-obnoxious Weasley brother who chooses the pursuit of power and service of a corrupt Ministry of Magic over his family and breaks his mother's heart. Yet, at the final reckoning against Voldemort, he shows up, astonished at first to blunder into Hogwarts and meet most of his family. But he quickly breaks the silence:

> "I was a fool," Percy roared. . . . "I was an idiot, I was a pompous prat, I was a—a—"
>
> "Ministry-loving, family-disowning, power-hungry moron," said Fred.
>
> Percy swallowed.
>
> "Yes, I was!"
>
> "Well, you can't say fairer than that," said Fred, holding out his hand to Percy. . . .
>
> "I'm sorry, Dad," Percy said.
>
> Mr. Weasley blinked rather rapidly, then he too hurried to hug his son.[41]

Percy's story has stretched across all seven volumes of the Harry Potter story: his early self-importance, his career climbing, his willingness to deny his family for advancement, his reluctance to see the growing darkness of the Ministry, his estrangement from those who still love him and want to see him become the person he is meant to be. But the shattering of the walls he has built comes about because he faces up to the person he has become and sees the many ways he had fallen short—sees them, and confesses them. Rowling described how "the new improved Percy" became an important part of positive change in the Wizarding world, and it all begins in this moment—with remorse and the desire to do better.[42]

Ron Weasley, too, demonstrates remorse, and it turns out that for once he needs to. When he deserts Harry and Hermione, leaving behind the quest for the Horcruxes, he breaks their fellowship—and their hearts. Although, as Rowling notes, Ron is neither the smartest nor the most skilled in the group, he is something else—"he held them together; his humour and his good heart were essential"—and his absence leaves his friends wandering.[43]

He has a change of heart, though, and at last, with the help of Dumbledore's Deluminator, he returns to them in a time of great need. He pulls Harry from the pool in the freezing Forest of Dean, destroys the locket Horcrux, and then, as if his actions did not say enough, he apologizes to Harry in cadences that seem to be endemic to the Weasley men:

> "I'm sorry," he said in a thick voice. "I'm sorry I left. I know I was a—a—"
> He looked around at the darkness, as if hoping a bad enough word would swoop down upon him and claim him.
> "You've sort of made up for it tonight," said Harry. "Getting the sword. Finishing off the Horcrux. Saving my life."[44]

Ron also tries to apologize to Hermione, although he at first has little success:

> "Oh, you're sorry! . . . You come back after weeks—weeks—and you think it's all going to be all right if you just say sorry?"
> "Well what else can I say?" Ron shouted.[45]

And indeed, what else is there to say, if you both mean it and if your life changes to show that you mean it? Remorse must be accompanied by amendment of life—the desire and active attempt to be different, to renounce past mistakes, misdeeds, and harmful actions and to replace them with just, loving, and selfless deeds.

The point of *metanoia* is not simply to leave behind the past, but to participate in the rescue of the present—and the future. And nowhere is this stirring possibility of remorse, return, and rebirth more powerfully illustrated than in the life of Albus Dumbledore. Although *Deathly Hallows* has enough action to fill any three books, it also contains a gripping mystery: *Who was the real Albus Dumbledore?* As the book progresses, Harry hears many stories about Dumbledore, from glowing tributes like the obituary

89

written by Elphias Doge, to scathing and scurrilous attacks from Auntie Muriel and Rita Skeeter, who writes an innuendo-filled biography, to the embittered comments of Albus' brother Aberforth, who still blames Albus for the death of their sister Ariana.

Harry's own discoveries too are disconcerting—over time he confirms that Dumbledore was, during his youth, the friend of the dark wizard Grindelwald, and that together, the two brilliant young wizards had hatched a plan to rule over Muggles—for "the greater good," as they put it. But there was a conflict between himself and Aberforth that drew all three wizards into a fight and, as a result—although Dumbledore did not intend it, and certainly mourned it for the rest of his life—Ariana was killed, Grindelwald fled, and Aberforth was ever after estranged from him. When Grindelwald went on to become a great and powerful dark wizard, employing their slogan "For the Greater Good" to justify his monstrous acts, while Dumbledore did not join his one-time friend—and later dueled and defeated him—it looked as though he bore some responsibility for the horror Grindelwald caused.

90 Harry wrestles with Rita Skeeter's accusations that Dumbledore's brilliant achievements, his hatred of the dark arts, his compassion toward Muggles, and his devotion to family were all a lie. The evidence seems daunting, and Dumbledore never shared with Harry anything of his own personal life that might serve to exonerate him. When Hermione tries to point out that Dumbledore made these mistakes when he was young, Harry bitterly replies, "'They were the same age we are now. And here we are, risking our lives to fight the Dark Arts, and there he was, in a huddle with his new best friend, plotting their rise to power over the Muggles.'"[46]

But Hermione defends Dumbledore—the Dumbledore they knew, the Dumbledore who had made such a positive difference in the world, the Dumbledore who had been a force for compassion, justice, and mercy—by speaking in the language of redemption:

> "He changed, Harry, he changed! It's as simple as that! Maybe he did believe these things when he was seventeen, but the whole of the rest of his life was devoted to fighting the Dark Arts! Dumbledore was the one who stopped Grindelwald, the one who

always voted for Muggle protection and Muggle-born rights, who fought You-Know-Who from the start, and who died trying to bring him down!"[47]

When we look at the fruits of Albus Dumbledore's life, perhaps we might discover some blighted branches or withered fruits: in pursuit of power, importance, and magical wisdom, in search of the Deathly Hallows, it may be true that he did not devote himself to the care of his brother and sister as he should have; entranced or infatuated by the brilliant, handsome, and dangerous Gellert Grindelwald, Dumbledore joined the young dark wizard in a serious quest for the Hallows and entered into the sort of interpersonal evil we have described earlier in which their fancies of power and control fed each other and the two discussed a future in which they would rule; in the argument with his brother that exploded into a wands-out three-way battle, Ariana was killed, perhaps even, as Dumbledore always feared, by himself.

These are undeniable acts worth repenting—but every indication is that, as Hermione argued, Dumbledore *did* repent. From the self-serving, self-centered, and power-seeking teenager who made these heartbreaking mistakes, he became a man who fought for the rights of the defenseless, the valiant leader of the battle against dark magic, and the one who knew how easy it is to commit evil or careless acts—and so behaved with forgiveness and tolerance, forgiving and offering the chance to repent to Snape and others. He became the man who marked his sister's grave with a reproach that became a reminder: "Where your treasure is, there will your heart be also." He became the greatest wizard of his age, the greatest headmaster in the history of Hogwarts School of Witchcraft and Wizardry, the man who willingly sacrificed everything up to and including his life for the sake of others. The fruits we witness in the life of Albus Dumbledore are overwhelmingly the fruits of a decent, loving, compassionate, and generous soul—exactly the Dumbledore we always believed we knew—and they are the fruits of repentance and renewal, of beautiful new life emerging from the imperfection of the old.

91

Deathly Hallows, as the climax to Harry's story, is filled with redemptions large and small: the final truth about Snape's true allegiance, and the story of his repentance—and his love; the rumor of Grindelwald's final remorse during his years of imprisonment; the movement of Kreacher from vile, muttering skulker to faithful and beloved servant; the discovery of Regulus Black's heroic secret turn from following the Dark Lord to attempting to destroy him; even the possibility of remorse offered to Voldemort himself, although that offer of redemption is snubbed.

When acted upon, though, remorse and amendment of life restore—or at least begin to restore—sundered souls, relationships, and institutions, and this is the subject of our final chapter. Harry Potter's story, as we have said, is about life and light, but it is about more than Harry's survival—or even the survival of those characters we have so loved through 4,100 pages. It is also about the coming of a new and better world. This is the world we witness in the final pages of *Harry Potter and the Deathly Hallows.*

And it is the world we work toward and hope to see ourselves someday.

4

All Was Well

Faith, Hope, and the World to Come

"The scar had not pained Harry for nineteen years. All was well."

—*Harry Potter and the Deathly Hallows*

"The last enemy that shall be destroyed is death."

—1 Corinthians 15:26, NRSV

J. K. Rowling: Christian Author?

In the spring of 2008, I was doing an interview with an evangelical British radio station about a book I had written on theology and film, and although my hosts and I clearly had some disagreements about belief and practice, our discussion was going pretty well. While I sometimes imagine that J. K. Rowling had in mind a certain kind of Christian when she named a character in the Harry Potter novels Pius Thicknesse, a name suggesting narrow piety, inflexibility, thick-headedness, and unquestioning belief, my hosts had proven to be surprisingly progressive. We made it past *Pulp Fiction*, with its violence, profanity, and sadism; past *American Beauty*, with its hedonism, drug use, and repressed homosexuality; past *Million Dollar Baby*, condemned by Catholic bishops for its acceptance of euthanasia as a possible solution to a life of paralysis and despair.

And then, it happened.

"What we don't understand," my host said, now moving to the attack, "is how you could make the mistake of writing anything positive about the Harry Potter films. Everyone knows that Harry Potter is Satanic, a passageway for kids to enter the study of the occult."

"Uhmm," I said, squirming a little. "I don't actually think that's true."

"No?" he said, more than a little surprised.

"No," I said, "After the final book came out, J. K. Rowling gave an interview to *Time* magazine in which she talked about how her Christian faith had informed the entire Harry Potter story. I've actually found it in earlier interviews, too. But she said she didn't want to draw too much attention to her faith because she was afraid people would be able to figure out how the story would end."

"Her faith?" he repeated, and again, you could see I was knocking on a door that had not been opened before. Never mind that when the final book came out, the London *Telegraph* had trumpeted this very fact: "J. K. Rowling: 'Christianity Inspired Harry Potter.'"

94

"Rowling is an active member of the Church of Scotland," I told him. "Her children have been christened. She talks openly about her Christianity. And when you look at the Potter story—especially now that the seventh novel has woven all the threads together—you can see how it has the same shape as the gospel story: sacrifice, death, resurrection, redemption."

There was a silence.

"I thought she was a witch," my host finally said, and while I sat there shaking my head, I also forgave him quickly, since I know this is not an uncommon assumption among Christians both in England and here in America. These rumors were all false, as we have noted, but Rowling herself addressed them from her earliest interviews:

I'm not a witch, she said. I'm a writer of children's fantasy.

I don't believe in magic, she told other interviewers. It's a device in my stories, nothing more.

I believe in God, she told others. I'm a Christian, actually, and I attend church more often than for weddings and funerals (and the head of the Church of Scotland has actually lauded the Potter books).[1]

Further than that, she for years refused to talk about her faith in interviews, saying that to do so might spoil the experience of readers. It was difficult to know exactly what this cryptic refusal might mean; some took her claims to religion as her attempt simply to defuse criticism. But at last, with the publication of the seventh and final novel, this enigmatic comment became clear: the Potter stories were ultimately about death and resurrection, sacrifice and salvation. They were, indeed, nothing more or less than a deeply Christian story about a prophesied savior who willingly and peacefully gives up his life to save the world, the Christian mythic narrative in fictional disguise.

So as Nancy Gibbs of *Time* magazine reported in 2007 (when *Time* chose Rowling as one of its People of the Year), the author's reticence to speak about her faith until after people had read *Harry Potter and the Deathly Hallows* revolved around her awareness of how the shape of the story she was writing matched the shape of the gospel narrative:

> Talk too much about her faith, [Rowling] feared, and it would become clear who would live and who would die and who might actually do both. After six books with no mention of God or Scripture, in the last book Harry discovers on his parents' graves a Bible verse that, Rowling says, is the theme for the entire series. It's a passage from I Corinthians in which Paul discusses Jesus' Resurrection: "The last enemy that shall be destroyed is death."[2]

Now, with the series concluded, Rowling has acknowledged how her faith shaped her writing of these books, how the shape of the Christian gospel and the shape of Harry's story are analogous, and how, according to Gibbs, "The biggest mystery [about the Potter books] appropriately, had to do with Rowling's own soul."[3] Rowling the supposed Satanist had, in Book 7, written the most clearly Christian ending one could imagine for her story, a story of hope and faith in the future—the anagogical dimension of her text.

Even before anyone thought of the Harry Potter novels as somehow Christian, Rowling's most obvious models had always been writers of Christian fantasy; as far back as 1999, Alison Lurie had written in the *New York Review of Books* that the Potter novels "belong to an ongoing tradition of Anglo-American fantasy that takes off from [J. R. R.] Tolkien and C. S. Lewis."[4] But with the publication of *Deathly Hallows*, it became impossible to ignore Rowling's dramatic use of Christian themes and the larger Christian narrative. *Christianity Today*, the most-read magazine of American evangelicals, published a review of *Deathly Hallows* which described it as deeply Christian, while as we noted, Lisa Miller wrote in *Newsweek* that Rowling's debt to the fantasy tradition and Christian mythos of writers like C. S. Lewis and J. R. R. Tolkien could not now be ignored.[5]

Now when I say that the Harry Potter novels may be taken seriously as Christian fiction, I should note immediately that I do not mean that Rowling intended for them to be evangelical or that she perceived them explicitly as vehicles for Christian meaning. Like their author, the Potter books are also reticent to speak about their faith. The Christian trappings of Rowling's universe, although the novels are set in our own world and in our present, are almost nonexistent. God is never directly discussed (although characters in *Goblet of Fire* say "My God," and "Good lord," for example, these uses are clearly cultural; by contrast, when Harry and Mrs. Weasley say "Thank God," in *Deathly Hallows* in response to the safety of those they love, it does seem to be a use of God's name in something like prayer). The name of Jesus Christ is never mentioned, and no character acknowledges him or herself to be a member of an established church, although Harry is said to have been christened, perhaps in the village church in Godric's Hollow where his parents are later buried, and we do hear the strains of Christmas carols coming from that church on Christmas Eve. Although Jeffrey Weiss has also argued for the Christian themes in the Potter books, he too suggests that "Harry's World is insistently devoid of explicit religion, right through the final chapter."[6] The Harry Potter saga, like many great books written by Christians, is not Christian because it depicts a recognizable Christian universe of faith and practice.

However, although I too think that Rowling is first and foremost an author of fine children's fantasy novels, not a Christian author in the limiting way we normally employ that term, Rowling's own awareness of the importance her faith has played in the structure and shape of the series suggests that we can discuss the books as Christian literature in a wider sense. Rowling has often mentioned her fondness for Graham Greene, and it is in the work of literary Christian authors like Greene, Walker Percy, Flannery O'Connor, and P. D. James (as well as in the obvious analogies we might make to those Christian fantasy authors C. S. Lewis, J. R. R. Tolkien, and George MacDonald) that we can turn for a greater understanding of how works may be written by a Christian author centering on themes and storylines drawn from the Christian tradition the author professes, yet appeal to a broad audience that may or may not share the author's faith commitment. In its attention to souls, mortality, redemption, good and evil, faith and belief, tolerance, and justice, the Harry Potter story is permeated with Rowling's faith. But one clearly does not have to share that faith to love the books.

C. S. Lewis himself once wrote that if Christian literature was understood, as it often is, to be "written by Christians for Christians," he had nothing much to say about it, and believed that perhaps nothing could be said.[7] For many years, "Christian literature" has meant literature in which art is subordinated to evangelical message, and unpleasant or unedifying details of everyday life supplanted (as in some of the revised *Tales of Beedle the Bard*) by wholesomeness, but given the fine authors in whose company I have placed Rowling, it should be clear that I am proposing a broader and deeper definition of Christian literature. Rowling certainly—and thankfully—is not writing to convert people (whether to Christianity or to witchcraft); she is only seeking to tell her story with as much joy and beauty and excitement as she can. But if we speak of a novel written by a Christian that employs Christian symbols and narrative tropes—particularly a novel that demonstrates the author's awareness that she is writing about a new world to come—while aiming at communicating with a wider audience, then I believe we begin to narrow in on the character of the work J. K. Rowling has done in the Harry Potter novels through an anagogical reading.

A great work of literature written by a religious writer can be recognized by its expert creation of a world equally coherent to all people, nonreligious people included, as Madeleine L'Engle, the Christian author of the much-loved children's novel *A Wrinkle in Time*, would concur. L'Engle, whose fantastic tales are also infused with her Christian belief, was, like Rowling, reluctant to be identified as too explicitly Christian in her work, saying, "I do not write my books for Christians . . . . If my stories are incomprehensible to Jews or Muslims or Taoists, then I have failed as a Christian writer. . . . If our lives are truly 'hid with Christ in God,' the astounding thing is that this hiddenness is revealed in all that we do and say and write. What we are is going to be visible in our art."[8]

And so, likewise, is J. K. Rowling's faith and practice evident in her own art, sometimes in ways that are less hidden. As Rowling mentioned in the 2007 *Time* interview, the New Testament verse on the Potters' graves about conquering death (1 Cor 15:26) is central to any understanding of Harry's story. Rowling in fact told reporters at a press conference for the release of the final book that both the scriptural quotations Harry finds on the tombstones at Godric's Hollow are important: "They sum up—they almost epitomize the entire series."[9] What might it mean when the author says that these two Bible verses—the only Bible verses directly quoted in these thousands of pages—sum up the Harry Potter story? A closer look reveals how her choice of verses sums up Christian faith and practice as well as summing up Harry's own fantastic journey.

The first of the two quotations found in *Deathly Hallows* is Matthew 6:21, a verse inscribed on the tomb of Albus' Dumbledore's sister Ariana: "Where your treasure is, there will your heart be also." This mention of treasure is not intended as some sort of financial advice, but (in common with much of the rest of the Gospel of Matthew) as "a radical challenge calling for the reorientation

98

of one's whole life."[10] It is about who we are, what we value, and what we seek.

The verse on James and Lily Potter's monument that causes Harry momentary consternation ("The last enemy to be destroyed is death") is from a section of the Apostle Paul's First Letter to the Corinthians where Paul discusses his understanding of resurrection and his faith that God's movement in the world is leading to the end of death and suffering. Richard B. Hays says that the sections of 1 Corinthians leading up to and including this verse are about the centrality of the resurrection to Christian faith: to deny the resurrection of Christ is to deny the gospel (literally, "the good news" or *evangelium*) of Christ, but because Christ has been raised from the dead, all who belong to him will likewise be raised.[11]

These two Bible verses, both perhaps chosen by Dumbledore (since Harry has no family members and no godfather available to select monument inscriptions) at once present us with a present-time theology (value what truly matters, because you will give your life to what you value) and an end-time theology (death is horrible but will someday be overcome). Together, the two constitute, as Rowling said, a recapitulation of the major themes of the Potter series—and an apt summary of the Christian faith. Live well now; hope for a better future.

So for Rowling to tell reporters that these two verses of Christian wisdom are the core of her story reiterate that she has written a deeply Christian story shaped by Christian faith, filled with Christian wisdom, and capable of opening valuable discussion on theological matters. As a novelist myself, I know that an author's intent (I am thinking specifically of Rowling's long-standing belief that Harry's tale mirrors the Christian narrative) does matter; artists have plans that are integrated with greater or lesser success into their work, and although they may not represent the only meanings that can emerge from a text, they are certainly conscious on the part of the artist. If J. K. Rowling says the Harry Potter novels were shaped by her faith, I think we need to listen to her, particularly since a four-fold reading of the text confirms the truth of that statement.

99

In concluding our discussion of the books, I want to consider important ways in which Rowling has retold elements of the Christian story, whether knowingly or unknowingly. She clearly had many of the elements of the good news in mind in telling Harry's good news (down to her insistence that after many years of believing the book should end with Harry's scar, at last she knew that the final sentence in the story would be "All was well," an echo of Dame Julian of Norwich's famous affirmation of Christian hope: "All shall be well, and all shall be well, and all manner of thing shall be well").[12] But in telling her story of the victory of love over hate, peace over violence, and life over death, J. K. Rowling may also have unknowingly tapped into many archetypal stories, characters, and themes that have relevance to the Christian story—and have found powerful expression in the fairy tales and fantasy of those writers who came before.

Fantasy, Fairy Tale, and Christian Epic

In addition to George MacDonald, C. S. Lewis, and J. R. R. Tolkien, fantasy novelists from whom we will hear more anon, recent years have also seen the publication of Philip Pullman's *His Dark Materials* trilogy. Although Pullman intentionally and aggressively attacks organized religion in these books, they are nonetheless powerfully theological; Rowan Williams has said on many occasions that despite these attacks, Pullman is one of his favorite writers, and he remarked in 2009 that he liked the Pullman novels precisely because they address theological questions like "human value, human depth, and three-dimensionality" with imagination at a time when theology has become less and less relevant to the intellectual mainstream.[13]

100

We have heard that fairy tales have the power to be moral without moralizing, and perhaps, we might say, to be theological without theologizing. Although she likes C. S. Lewis' *The Chronicles of Narnia*, Rowling herself is adamant that her work is intended to be moral without moralizing. As she told *Time*'s Nancy Gibbs,

> "I did not set out to convert anyone to Christianity. I wasn't trying to do what C. S. Lewis did. It is perfectly possible to live a very moral life without a belief in God, and I think it's perfectly

possible to live a life peppered with ill-doing and believe in God." And now she climbs into a pulpit of her own, and you can tell how much this all matters to her, if it weren't already clear from her 4,100-page treatise on tolerance. "I'm opposed to fundamentalism in any form," she says. "And that includes in my own religion."[14]

While Lewis (who is not around to defend himself) might disagree with whether the Chronicles were written to convert readers, both he and Rowling would agree on the power of story to allow morals to creep past waiting dragons. Indeed, some would tell us that if we are going to understand Christianity, we may only do it through story. The life of Jesus, which we understand first as story, is our surest guide to what it is that Christianity is about; Origen said that Jesus is the kingdom of God in the shape of a human life. Likewise, our own understanding comes best through story, so that as we read the Harry Potter novels, we are reminded of what is good and real and true by seeing those qualities—and their opposites— lived out as the stories of human lives. Stanley Hauerwas suggested that those stories that shape us and move us will necessarily be adventure stories, and we have affirmed that those adventures may necessarily contain things that are dark and challenging. Rowan Williams notes in *Grace and Necessity* that "doing justice to the physical world . . . is reflecting the love of God for it, the fact that this world is worth dying for in God's eyes."[15] If this is true, then to leave out the dark and difficult corners of creation is both unartistic and actually un-Christian. As we saw in our discussion of fairy tales, the happy ending—the hope we recognize as the anagogical dimension of a story—is a direct correlative to the deepness of the darkness before the coming of the light.

In such a story, we look for—and gratefully experience—Tolkien's eucatastrophe when what looked hopeless turns into a world suffused with hope. Tolkien suggested that the birth of Jesus marked the eucatastophe of the human story, and the resurrection, the eucatastophe of the story of God's incarnation. In doing so, Tolkien marked how the fairy tale and the tale of the life of Jesus Christ are alike—and how the Christian narrative is perhaps a source for

101

such endings of hope and joy. Ultimately, he says, sudden joyful reversal is not about escape from the grim realities and heartbreaks that have followed or the death that threatens, but "a sudden and miraculous grace" that does not deny the reality of sorrow, failure, and death, since "the possibility of these is necessary to the joy of deliverance." Eucatastrophe does not deny the hardships that have come before; it does, however, deny their final victory and, Tolkien said, "in so far is *evangelium* [good news], giving a fleeting glimpse of Joy, Joy beyond the walls of the world, poignant as grief."[16] Christians too believe in happy endings, as much as the story up to that point might militate against it, as horrific as the events in the story to that point might have been. "The meaning of stories," theologian John Polkinghorne writes, in words that could easily be Tolkien's, "lies in their endings, an insight that points to the significance of the future. The prevalence of 'happy endings' is not mere sentimentality, but an insight of eschatological hopefulness that in the end, all shall be well."[17] We dwell, not on the scars, but on the hope.

Like Rowling, George MacDonald, C. S. Lewis, and J. R. R. Tolkien all wrote fantasy epics in which the church seems absent as an institution, yet in each of their greatest stories, the Christian story lies submerged just below the surface and sometimes breaking through into the light. In discussing MacDonald's work, Lewis wrote that this sort of mythic fantasy "gets under our skin, hits us at a level deeper than our thoughts or even our passions, troubles oldest certainties till all questions are reopened, and in general shocks us more fully awake than we are for most of our lives."[18] In Lewis' *Chronicles of Narnia*, long recognized as a Christian epic, there is a Deeper Magic beyond the events of the day, more powerful and fundamental than the magic of the White Witch and the conflict between her forces and the forces of Good, and it is in that Deeper Magic that the spiritual content bubbles, teaching us as we follow the story what is to be desired and where we should find our treasures. Tolkien, meanwhile, wrote of a world menaced by the Ultimate Evil—and somehow, by the power of love and sacrifice, rescued from oblivion. Speaking of fairy stories (although he could have been writing of his own fantasy epic), he wrote that "in such stories when the sudden *turn* comes we get a piercing glimpse of joy, and heart's desire, that for a moment passes outside the frame, rends indeed the very web of story, and lets a gleam come through."[19] That gleam, we might say, is of the Deeper Magic beyond the veil.

Like Tolkien and Lewis, J. K. Rowling wrote a voluminous fairy tale about how, in the end, all shall be well, something essentially Christian, in which she affixed a powerful eucatastophe to a story in which it looked as though evil and death would carry the day. We might also say that J. K. Rowling wrote a serious story about the power of death—and about the much greater power of love. In its final reversal of death and despair through hope and love, the Potter story reminds us how well-written tales of the fantastic often have the power to reteach us the Christian story, how in Tolkien's words, they presage some deep Joy beyond the bounds of the story we have been reading.

At the end of things, despite the dangers and difficulties before us now, all will be well.

Bob Smietana marked in *Christianity Today* how with the seventh Harry Potter novel, Rowling began to show even the doubters that, as in C. S. Lewis' Narnia, "her world has a 'deeper magic.'"[20] Beyond the charms and jinxes and even the Unforgiveable Curses, there is a magic that lies at the heart of creation, a magic more powerful than any that humans can wield. It is the deeper magic that emerges unaccountably when Lily Potter offers her life to save her child; it is the deeper magic that shatters Voldemort's power then and in the end, when Harry repeats his mother's sacrifice. It is the deeper magic that binds friends like Ron, Hermione, and Harry together in the face of death. It is the deeper magic that allows Dumbledore to go knowingly to his own death with the intent of preserving a student from an act that would destroy his soul. It is the deeper magic that allows a villain such as Snape to be redeemed—and even permits that possibility for a villain such as Voldemort, if he would only show remorse, and seek redemption.

Like Voldemort in his final battle with Harry, we could, I suppose, sneer at this point and ask, "Is it love again?"[21]

But in the Christian story, as in Harry's story, this is what it ultimately comes down to: Love is the deeper magic of the world. It was love that created us, love that redeemed us, love that sacrificed all for us, love that loves us still—and will always love us. Madeleine L'Engle concluded that love is the essential ingredient of any Christian story, children's or otherwise, and the Harry Potter story gets this absolutely right.[22]

Christian Belief and the Potter Novels

We have already debunked the bad literal reading that Rowling's books teach belief in magic, but that does not mean that her work doesn't have a great deal to say about belief. Because of her use of mythic and sacred archetypes, and her sense of the power of community, Rowling's characters—particularly Dumbledore and the trinity of Harry, Ron, and Hermione—can teach us much about the central element of Christian belief: that we believe in one God, Father, Son, and Holy Spirit.

And perhaps the story can also help us to understand belief wrongly applied; in her introduction of the Deathly Hallows and the idea of a faithful pursuit of them, Rowling descibes something that might be a parody of religious faith—or a depiction of misplaced belief. The possessor of all three of the Hallows—the Wand of Destiny, the Cloak, the Resurrection Stone—is said to become the Master of Death, and over the generations, some wizards have given their lives to the pursuit of knowledge about the Hallows—or to the pursuit of the Hallows themselves. As Xenophilius Lovegood says, he is not surprised to have to enlighten Harry and the others about the Hallows. "You haven't heard of them? I'm not surprised. Very, very few wizards believe. . . . Such ignorance. There is nothing Dark about the Hallows—at least, not in that crude sense. One simply uses the symbol to reveal oneself to other believers, in the hope that they might help one with the Quest."[23]

Like Christians, Jews, and other people of faith, seekers of the Deathly Hallows recognize each other by a symbol, the triangular eye, and a community of sorts has grown up around their individual quests for meaning. The pursuit of the Hallows is described as a

104

journey of faith; one either believes or one doesn't. Pursuers of the Hallows have a set of "scriptures" in the "Tale of the Three Brothers" in the *Tales of Beedle the Bard*, which they interpret as being a children's story that retells the elements of their belief (perhaps sneaking past the dragons of disbelief). They also have a set of founders, the Peverell brothers, who they believe to be the initiators of their faith—the first possessors of the Deathly Hallows.

Followers of the Hallows thus have a practice that mimics religion, and a belief in something beyond themselves that mimics faith. As Dumbledore and Harry both discover, though, this Way is ultimately more about acquiring personal power than it is about surrender to a transcendental Power, and even without Dumbledore's postmortem apologies to Harry for his pursuit of the Hallows, perhaps the simple fact that the Hallows' most prominent follower in the Potter tale is the more than slightly off-balance Xenophilius Lovegood should be sufficient to notify us that this faith system falls short. When Hermione asks how the Resurrection Stone can be real, Xeno's response is short and instructive: "Prove that it is not."[24]

Xenophilius' daughter Luna is likewise an ardent believer in many unseen things, often without or despite the evidence. This too could fit the well-known definition of faith established by the book of Hebrews ("Now faith is the assurance of things hoped for, the conviction of things not seen," Heb 11:1, NRSV), although there may be some important points to draw from Luna's example. As Rowling notes, Luna is a sort of anti-Hermione: "Hermione's so logical and inflexible in so many ways and Luna is likely to believe 10 impossible things before breakfast."[25] Some of those things (such as Luna's belief that Harry did witness Voldemort's return) turn out to be true. Others (such as the existence of the Crumple-Horned Snorkack) seem less likely to be worthy of belief. Perhaps Xeno and Luna might represent for us the spiritual necessity of discernment; what one believes may be more important than how fervently one believes it. Jesus spoke in the Gospel of Matthew about a foolish man who built his home on an unstable foundation, and how when the winds and rain came, they leveled the house (Matt 7:26-27). John Chrysostom, preaching on this same passage, said, "He was right in calling this one a fool; because what could be more brain-less than building a house on the sand? For such a one endures the work of building but deprives oneself of one's labor and of relaxation, experiencing punishment instead of benefit."[26] This is dramatically illustrated when the Erumpent Horn at the Lovegoods' (which Xeno believes—stubbornly, ardently—to be the horn of a Crumple-Horned Snorkack) explodes and almost blows the house up. Wrong belief can be as damaging as believing nothing, perhaps more so.

Rowling has said repeatedly that she doesn't believe in magic ("I do believe in other kinds of magic; the magic of the imagination, for example, and love, but magic as in waving a wand—no"), and her story itself proves that magic is not the belief system she values.[27] It is, however, about the deep-seated things she does believe. On the same *Potterwatch* broadcast that witnesses Kingsley Shacklebolt's call to our common humanity, Remus Lupin, Harry's old Defense against the Dark Arts teacher, reminds listeners that Harry repre-sents everything that matters: "'The Boy Who Lived' remains a sym-bol of everything for which we are fighting: the triumph of good, the power of innocence, the need to keep resisting."[28] It could be a checklist for the life of faith; if rebels in first-century Palestine had broadcast a radio show, these words might perhaps have been spoken of Jesus.

Harry is a potent symbol for Remus and the others because he stands for so many transcendent values, and in the Harry Potter saga, he takes on a distinctly messianic tinge, although Harry is far from the only character who seems to represent Christian arche-types. Albus Dumbledore, Ron, and Hermione also at times seem to incarnate Christian beliefs about the Creator of the Universe, the Savior of Humankind, and the Spirit of Love—what we know as the Triune God of Christianity. In the lives and actions of these characters, we can see many of the central truths of the Christian faith brought to dramatic life.

Some of these associations are conscious on Rowling's part. As we have seen, the author spoke early on about how Harry's story cleaved so closely to the gospel narrative that she didn't want to reveal too much about her own faith for fear it would also reveal her ending; depicting a character like Harry who is prophesied to save his people, who is called "The Chosen One," and who ultimately chooses to sacrifice his own life to bring about life for all certainly implies that we are supposed to view him as a Christ figure. Other similarities, of course, may be unintentional, simply a natural byproduct of telling a story where love triumphs over death and community creates powerful meaning for those who participate in it. But by examining these elements, we will find powerful dramatic illustrations of the creedal Christian truths: *We believe in God the Father . . . God the Son . . . God the Holy Spirit.*

First, and most obviously, Rowling presents Harry Potter as a Christ figure. Many, if not most, of these similarities seem to be consciously chosen by Rowling for their powerful associations. In comparing Harry to Jesus Christ, incidentally, we do not intend blasphemy, but simply to assess the ways in which Harry is a literary Christ figure; we are not saying that Harry *is* Jesus, but that in important respects he is *like* Jesus. There are also, of course, many ways in which Harry is not like Jesus: Lily Potter was not reputed to be a virgin when she gave birth to Harry; Jesus (so far as is recorded in any of the extant gospels) did not play Quidditch or enjoy Fizzing Whizbees. But it is the similarities, not the obvious differences, of the two that may help us to better understand Jesus and Christian belief, and so it is to those similarities we turn.

Although Harry is not born of a virgin, as described in the gospels of Matthew and Luke, we can certainly note elements of the miraculous about his birth and first appearance in the world of the books. Harry, of course, is the subject of prophecy. Before his birth, Sibyll Trelawney, in a rare moment of true far-seeing, announces to Dumbledore that "THE ONE WITH THE POWER TO VANQUISH THE DARK LORD APPROACHES . . . BORN TO THOSE WHO HAVE THRICE DEFIED HIM, BORN AS THE SEVENTH MONTH DIES."[29] A Christian understanding of Jesus' birth includes the idea that the Hebrew Scriptures predicted that God would send a savior, a messiah, to liberate his people, and that Jesus was that predicted savior. Moreover, in the Gospel of Matthew, a

107

group of astrologers examining the conjunction of the stars travel to Palestine to find the king their sky-gazing has predicted: "In the time of King Herod, after Jesus was born in Bethlehem of Judea, wise men from the East came to Jerusalem, asking, 'Where is the child who has been born king of the Jews? For we observed his star at its rising, and have come to pay him homage'" (Matt 2:1-2, NRSV). The centaurs in the Forbidden Forest likewise have read the heavenly bodies and discovered a message concerning Harry. The centaur Bane says of Harry, "Have we not read what is to come in the movement of the planets?"[30]

Like Jesus, Harry survives an attempt on his life during his infancy from a power who believes his birth could end his reign. In the gospel narrative, King Herod hears with some dismay the news of the astrologers from the East who have come to venerate the King of the Jews the skies have prophesied. When they fail to return to tell him where to find this king, Herod reacts violently to protect his throne. The Gospel of Matthew recounts that "When Herod saw that he had been tricked by the wise men, he was infuriated, and he sent and killed all the children in and around Bethlehem who were two years old or under, according to the time that he had learned from the wise men" (Matt 2:16, NRSV). Similarly, when Lord Voldemort hears the prophecy that a child of his opponents born at the end of July will be his doom, he takes violent action. Singling out Harry Potter (although the prophecy might also refer to Neville Longbottom), he attacks the Potters and tries to kill Harry so that the prophecy may be overthrown.

The correspondences between Jesus and Harry Potter continue past their births and early childhoods. Most strikingly, we find the idea that both are somehow chosen—and yet that those to whom they come misunderstand their missions. Jesus is followed by disciples, welcomed into the royal city of Jerusalem by adoring throngs, but he is also insulted, reviled, and ultimately killed. Harry, for his part, is famous in the Wizarding world from his infancy, The Boy Who Lived, and later many in the Wizarding world take up the cry that he is The Chosen One, the only one who can redeem them from the evil of Voldemort and his followers. But Harry is also

108

insulted; he is accused of seeking publicity by publicity hound Gilderoy Lockhart, by Dolores Umbridge, and by the *Daily Prophet*, the Wizarding newspaper, which turns him into a running joke after he tries to warn that You-Know-Who has returned.

Hermione summarizes for Harry how the *Prophet* has treated him:

> "They're writing about you as though you're this deluded, attention-seeking person who thinks he's a great tragic hero or something. . . . They keep slipping in snide comments about you. If some far-fetched story appears they say something like 'a tale worthy of Harry Potter' and if anyone has a funny accident or anything it's 'let's hope he hasn't got a scar on his forehead or we'll be asked to worship him next—' "[31]

The gospels record similar stories about Jesus returning to Nazareth, his hometown, and how people were outraged by his teaching and speaking, and even insult him by suggesting he is a bastard child (instead of the child of a miraculous conception). In the Gospel of Luke's rendering of the story, the people listening to Jesus "sprang to their feet and hustled him out of the town; and they took him up to the brow of the hill their town was built on, intending to throw him off the cliff" (Luke 4:29, NJB). It's not surprising that in all the versions of this story Jesus recites a familiar wisdom saying of the Greco-Roman world: that the prophet (or savior) is not recognized in his hometown.

109

Jesus and Harry are also alike in the roles people expect them to play—although those people are all expecting the wrong thing. The Jews awaiting their messiah expected that he would be someone who would overthrow the Roman occupation government—a new King David sent by God to physically redeem them. But Jesus did not come to fight against the physical powers of the world, and the crowds screaming "Hosanna" in the streets of Jerusalem at the beginning of Holy Week on Palm Sunday had turned to crowds shouting "Crucify him" by Good Friday. What they did not understand was that Jesus was not a martial hero, and that his kingdom was not an earthly kingdom; instead, God would turn his submission and sacrifice into genuine victory, not over physical armies, but over the human enemies: fear, death, and hopelessness.

Harry and the Salvation of the World

Those in the Wizarding world—even his friends and supporters—misunderstand Harry as well, and this can be seen most clearly in the last two books. After Harry and members of Dumbledore's Army face down Voldemort and the Death Eaters at the Ministry of Magic, the belief that Harry is The Chosen One spreads far and wide. People believe that Harry is a powerful magician who can go toe-to-toe with He-Who-Must-Not-Be-Named, but while Harry is a brave and talented wizard, he is not the demigod people imagine. When at the beginning of *Deathly Hallows* Harry's wand fights off Voldemort in the escape from Little Whinging, Harry knows that this escape was not his doing, even though everyone else thinks that Harry has stood off Voldemort again through the force of his magic. Likewise, when Harry, Ron, and Hermione go on the run in *Deathly Hallows* in search of the Horcruxes, Ron and Hermione seem to expect him to be prepared to encounter the challenges ahead of them, and they are startled to discover that Harry has no idea what to do, no plan, no secret knowledge. "'We thought you knew what you were doing!' shouted Ron . . . 'We thought Dumbledore had told you what to do, we thought you had a real plan!'"[32]

At *Potterwatch* and among the reassembled Dumbledore's Army, people are awaiting Harry's instructions and leadership, waiting for the revolution. When Harry, Ron, and Hermione return to Hogwarts, Neville, who has been organizing resistance in Harry's name, turns to Harry with anticipation:

> "Everyone in here's proven they're loyal to Dumbledore—loyal to you," Neville says. "We all thought that if you came back it would mean revolution. That we were going to overthrow Snape and the Carrows."
>
> "Of course that's what it means," Luna Lovegood adds. "Isn't it, Harry? We're going to fight them out of Hogwarts?"
>
> But Harry tells them, "That's not what we came back for."[33]

110

His mission does not revolve around standing up to the Death Eaters in combat, and his contradiction of those who don't understand his true mission echoes the frequent response of Jesus to those who misunderstand him. On many occasions, followers or opponents think they know what he's all about, but Jesus corrects them. In the Gospel of Matthew, we find him teaching about God's kingdom on a mountain, but cautioning the assembled crowds, "Do not think that I have come to abolish the law or the prophets; I have come not to abolish but to fulfill" (Matt 5:17, NRSV). He responds to criticism of his compassionate association with the dregs of society by telling his critics, "Go and learn what this means, 'I desire mercy, not sacrifice.' For I have come to call not the righteous but sinners" (Matt 9:13, NRSV).

Jesus is constantly misunderstood, since his purpose is spiritual rather than martial, but that doesn't mean that Jesus didn't understand the call to physical pleasures and power. Before the start of his public ministry, the gospel story records that Satan tempted Jesus with power, glory, and fame—with all those things our world holds important. Like Jesus, who was tempted to enjoy and employ earthly power, Harry also wrestles with the temptation of temporal things. After Harry learns about the Deathly Hallows, for example, he obsesses for long weeks over these three objects that would give him control over death. He particularly covets the Elder Wand, the most powerful wand in existence; it might even give him the chance to face down Voldemort in a fair fight. But at last it becomes clear to Harry that he cannot and should not try to fight Lord Voldemort—that, like Jesus, only through submission and sacrifice can he defeat a brutal ruling power.

Jesus was invited to become a worldly liberator, an invitation he declined; he was not that kind of messiah, as we've noted. Jesus chooses to come as the Prince of Peace, not as a warrior king, and he not only refuses to ascend to power through violence, he even declines the chance to defend himself against violence with violence. The writer of the Gospel of Matthew records the capture of Jesus while he is at prayer and his refusal to defend himself—or to be defended:

111

Now the betrayer had given them a sign, saying, "The one I will kiss is the man; arrest him." At once he came up to Jesus and said, "Greetings, Rabbi!" and kissed him.

Jesus said to him, "Friend, do what you are here to do." Then they came and laid hands on Jesus and arrested him.

Suddenly, one of those with Jesus put his hand on his sword, drew it, and struck the slave of the high priest, cutting off his ear.

Then Jesus said to him, "Put your sword back into its place; for all who take the sword will perish by the sword. Do you think that I cannot appeal to my Father, and he will at once send me more than twelve legions of angels? But how then would the scriptures be fulfilled, which say it must happen in this way?"

At that hour Jesus said to the crowds, "Have you come out with swords and clubs to arrest me as though I were a bandit? Day after day I sat in the temple teaching, and you did not arrest me. But all this has taken place, so that the scriptures of the prophets may be fulfilled." Then all the disciples deserted him and fled. (Matt 26:48-56, NRSV)

112   Although Jesus says that he could return violence for violence, he chooses not to; this is not part of God's design, represented by the prophecies he mentions. However we understand the crucifixion of Jesus, Christians believe it comes as part of God's plan to right the world. My theology professor Tony Baker, in discussing Hans Urs von Balthasar's views of Jesus' death in *A Theology of History*, once told us that the crucifixion and resurrection of Jesus is God rewriting the ending to a story that otherwise would end badly— here is the eucatastophe Tolkien spoke of, written by God.[34] Jesus, however, has to acquiesce to that sacrificial ending, since it is his life on the line.

Likewise, as counterintuitive and countercultural as it might seem to us, Harry's way to rewrite an ending that does not bode well for humankind is to die willingly at Voldemort's hands rather than resisting him. He has sought power to overthrow the Dark Lord, particularly in his quest for the Deathly Hallows, but Harry comes to understand that he is no match for Voldemort. He has survived trial after trial, not purely through luck or more talented friends, as Voldemort accuses, but with the awareness that his skills are well suited to some trials—not including a head-to-head battle against the greatest dark wizard of all time. So it is that when Harry learns from Snape's memories of the Deeper Magic that will defeat Voldemort—but that will require his walking to offer himself to death—he recognizes that it is the right, the only choice: "These thoughts pattered against the hard surface of the incontrovertible truth, which was that he must die. *I must die.* It must end."[35]

In that death—and resurrection—Harry's story most clearly conforms to that of Christ's. In the Gospel of John, Jesus succinctly lays out the dimensions of what he will be doing. "Love one another," he first commands his followers, "as I have loved you." And then Jesus explains what form that love might take: "No one can have greater love than to lay down his life for his friends" (John 15:12-13, paraphrase). Rowling said of the ending to *Deathly Hallows,* "I wanted to show [Harry] loving. Sometimes it's dramatic: it means you lay down your life."[36] This is the love that Harry's mother Lily demonstrated, love that ended up saving her son and blasting Voldemort into powerlessness. And this is also what Harry does when he walks into the Forbidden Forest intending to allow Voldemort to kill him. As Jeffrey Weiss noted, the great clue "to the Christian nature of the Potter saga . . . is a theme that Ms. Rowling introduced in the very first book: The greatest power in Harry's World turns out to be the substitutionary sacrifice of one's life, when offered only for love, and with no hope of survival."[37]

Substitutionary atonement, the idea that Jesus died in place of humanity in order to save humanity, is a mainstream Christian understanding, and Harry's substitutionary sacrifice—and later resurrection and victory over death—is clearly linked to that of Jesus Christ. While Harry's death and resurrection don't bring eternal life in the cosmic sense that Jesus' did, they still offer life, as Harry explains to Voldemort after his return from King's Cross: "You won't be able to kill any of them ever again. . . . I meant to [die], and that's what did it. I've done what my mother did. They're protected from you."[38] Because Harry went willingly to his death, he

saved those he loved and eventually, through the defeat of Voldemort, the entire world.

This death that Harry chose so no one else need die is a dramatic rendering of Christian belief. Not all Christians, however,
understand the death of Christ to be simply substitutionary, as a
ransom, or to redeem those condemned to die. Jesus' life and death
may also be meaningful as a model of perfect love and submission
to God. Rowan Williams has written that Jesus models a human life
that is so infused with the purposes of God that people speak of it
as God's life "'translated' into another medium"; it is an example
of a human life perfectly attuned to God's purposes.[39] The medieval
theologian Peter Abelard imagined that this example of Jesus' faithful life and death could reshape us into people willing to be more
like him, to unite our human nature to the divine will in perfect
love.[40] Because Jesus adopted human form, he represented a model
we could—and should—follow.

But just as the life of Jesus inspires people to be Christ-like, we
might say that Harry's life and death stir people to be Harry-like,
to be brave and selfless and strong in the face of evil. This is what
Lupin was talking about on the Wizarding Wireless, and it is what
Colin Creevey, Ginny Weasley, and all the vast throng flocking back
to the final battle against Voldemort and the Death Eaters indicate:
Harry's example is an inspiration that invites people to participate
in that which most needs doing. In a review of *Deathly Hallows*, my
friend Ken Cuthbertson writes,

> As I read the deeper magic of Joanne Rowling, she is dealing
> with the aspect of Christianity that reminds us that we are not
> just called to "believe" in Jesus as the Christ. Rather, we are
> called and graced to become "little Christs" participating in
> the redemption of the world. That is to say that Harry fulfills the
> ancient magic that is supposed to be the outcome of baptism,
> our christening.[41]

We can see this ancient magic most dramatically at work in the
life of Neville Longbottom, who becomes perhaps the most Harry-
like of characters in a saga full of people transformed by the example

of The Boy Who Lived. When we first meet Neville in *Philosopher's Stone*, he is presented as a blunderer and a buffoon who can't keep track of his toad and who melts a cauldron into a twisted lump of metal in his first potions class. By the time the year has finished, though, he has learned enough bravery to stand up to Harry, Ron, and Hermione to try to keep them from sneaking out at night and losing any more points for Gryffindor in the House Cup competition. While Neville remains something of a clown in succeeding years, he watches Harry, Ron, and Hermione, and he continues to change. He develops a skill for herbology (eventually he will become a Hogwarts professor), he takes over Dumbledore's Army in Harry's absence, showing great courage, and at last, when he believes that Voldemort has killed Harry, he attacks the Dark Lord himself. Disarmed by the Dark Lord, Neville stands up to him just as Harry had—and will again. When Voldemort offers to spare his life if he will join him, Neville says, "I'll join you when hell freezes over," and shouts "Dumbledore's Army!"[42]

And then, moments later, he, like Harry before him, draws the sword of Godric Gryffindor from the Sorting Hat, and he cuts off the head of Nagini, Voldemort's monstrous pet snake and the final Horcrux, making it possible for Harry then to defeat Voldemort forever.

Neville's movement from hapless Harry-follower to someone who is Harry-like illustrates the transformation of human beings who aspire to follow the example of Christ; the potential for new life emerges from Harry's own life and sacrifice. Whether one believes in the miracle of substitutionary sacrifice or the power of an exemplary life—or both—the important thing is that in the life, death, and resurrection of Jesus Christ now human life has the possibility of real meaning. As N. T. Wright says of the resurrection,

> When Jesus rose again God's whole new creation rose from the tomb, introducing a world full of new potential and possibility. Indeed precisely because part of that new possibility is for human beings themselves to be revived and renewed, the resurrection of Jesus doesn't leave us as passive, helpless spectators. We find ourselves lifted up, set up on our feet, given new breath in our

115

lungs, and commissioned to go and make new creation happen in the world.[43]

This sounds precisely like the ending of Book 7, when all who witness Harry's death and rebirth join together to bring new life to the world, a subject we will explore in our conclusion.

Harry is a savior, because within the confines of Rowling's story, in a very real sense he does destroy death, as the pivotal biblical inscription in the Godric's Hollow graveyard said, as Jesus is said to have done in our world, and the use of Jesus' story within Harry's story is powerful. But there are other ways in which the Potter novels illuminate Christian faith, one of them being a very tangible understanding of the central Christian belief about Trinity communicated by the trio of Harry, Ron, and Hermione, and represented by Dumbledore.

Trinity and Unity

Christians understand the three members of the Trinity to make up a unity, with each member of the Trinity expressed in a distinct fashion—and at the same time, each giving and returning love, making the work of the others possible and tangible. Ron, Hermione, and Harry are presented in the books as three people who are at the same time distinct individuals and a unity; whenever someone suggests that Harry has accomplished all he has done by himself, he quickly returns that he has had help from his friends, and this trinity is indeed at the heart of all the good recorded in Rowling's novels, from the very beginning. In *Philosopher's Stone*, each of the three has qualities necessary to bypass the obstacles in their way: Harry's flying skills, Ron's chess acumen, and Hermione's logic deliver Harry to his final confrontation with Quirrell/Voldemort. Throughout the series, with rare exceptions, all three are on hand at climactic moments, and never is the necessity of trinity more clear than when one member is missing, as in *Chamber of Secrets*, when Hermione is removed from action and Harry and Ron must blunder to a solution, or in *Deathly Hallows*, when Ron departs the group for a time and Hermione and Harry are left to wander aimlessly without him, the silence growing between them.

Although we have seen that Harry is often presented as a Christ figure, I do not wish to suggest that we ought to view Rowling's trinity in simple terms of Father, Son, and Spirit—none of these three, for example, seems a likely candidate for God the Father—but Hermione, Ron, and Harry can help us think about theological attributes of the Trinity. It has been said that in the Holy Trinity, we see God at work in Thought, Action, and Emotion, and these do seem to have easy correspondences in our Potter trinity. Hermione, who can quote endlessly from *A History of Hogwarts* and who constantly employs cool logic ("Don't be so stupid," is her constant admonition), might represent Thought; Harry, who is relentlessly in motion, the Seeker in word and in deed, might represent Action; Ron, who experiences every feeling in a big way, whether fear of spiders or jealousy over Hermione, might be Emotion. Together the three work together, prop up each other, and accomplish what needs to be done.

This trio is not the only place in the Potter stories where we might find aspects of the Trinity. Some characters can be profitably compared to one or more persons of the Trinity. Hagrid, for all his blundering and mead-swilling, would make, for example, a really ripping Holy Spirit, powerful and nurturing and supportive; so would Mrs. Weasley. But it is the figure of the multivalenced Albus Percival Wulfric Brian Dumbledore who may represent our best picture of how the multiple persons of God operate in orthodox Christian belief, since Dumbledore illustrates the identities of each member of the Trinity at one time or another, from God the Father to God the Son to God the Holy Spirit.

An obvious role for Dumbledore in the Potter saga is that of God the Father. He even looks the part of God, at least as God is often depicted in Western sacred art: powerful, white-bearded, wise, an authority figure. God is depicted as the First Mover, whose wishes shape reality, and while neither all-knowing nor all-powerful, Dumbledore certainly represents the force behind the scenes throughout the Potter saga, the one who knows (mostly) everything going on, the one planning and orchestrating the action. In Book 1, for example, we see that, despite Professor McGonagall's objections, he plans to leave Harry with his Muggle relatives (in Book 3, Hagrid reveals, for example, that Harry's godfather Sirius wished to take Harry—"'Give Harry ter me, Hagrid, I'm his godfather, I'll look after him' . . . But I'd had me orders from Dumbledore . . . Harry was to go ter his aunt an' uncle's").[44]

When Harry returns to Hogwarts, Dumbledore returns his father's invisibility cloak to him, a magical gift instrumental to many of the adventures Harry, Ron, and Hermione undertake, beginning in *Philosopher's Stone* and extending into Harry's pursuit of Horcruxes and Hallows in *Deathly Hallows*; he also, unbeknownst to any of the characters (and many readers), sets Severus Snape to watch Harry and protect him, a protection that Harry fails to perceive because of Snape's clear distaste for him. After Voldemort returns in *Goblet of Fire*, Dumbledore orchestrates all that happens afterward. He tasks Harry with the investigation and destruction of Lord Voldemort's Horcruxes, the dark artifacts the Dark Lord has used to split his soul in hopes of preserving his life. And, to even Snape's surprise, Dumbledore plans, at the proper time, to sacrifice his most-beloved student, Harry, since it is the only way that Voldemort's evil can be vanquished.[45]

Harry, however, is more accepting of this design:

> Of course there had been a bigger plan; Harry had simply been too foolish to see it, he realized that now. . . . How neat, how elegant, not to waste any more lives, but to give the dangerous task to the boy who had already been marked for slaughter, and whose death would not be a calamity, but another blow against Voldemort.[46]

In this plan, Dumbledore perhaps most resembles the Christian God, who is said to love the world so greatly, desire its redemption so powerfully, that any sacrifice is worthwhile. A familiar section of the Gospel of John says that "God so loved the world that he gave his only Son, so that everyone who believes in him may not perish but may have eternal life. Indeed, God did not send the Son into the world to condemn the world, but in order that the world might be saved through him" (John 3:16-17, NRSV). Truly, Harry is precious to Dumbledore, as the headmaster reveals (readers had long

118

known as much) at the end of *Order of the Phoenix*. After Voldemort's return and Sirius' death, Dumbledore finally told Harry that
he had put off telling him that he would ultimately have to face
Voldemort because he wanted to spare Harry that horrifying news:

> "I cared about you too much," Dumbledore said simply. "I cared
> more for your happiness than for your knowing the truth, more
> for your peace of mind than my plan, more for your life than the
> lives that might be lost if the plans failed. In other words, I acted
> exactly as Voldemort expects we fools who love to act."[47]

But at last, because of his love for the world, because it is the
only way to redeem the world, Dumbledore is willing to sacrifice
his "son" Harry; only through Harry's willing death, Dumbledore
knows, can evil and death be vanquished and love made ascendant.

Dumbledore is not distinguished merely by his desire to shape
the action—Voldemort also has schemes and plots, as we presume
do Cornelius Fudge and Rufus Scrimgeour—but all of the plans
Dumbledore hatches are launched out of love and hope and the
desire that even the most bumbling or depraved of beings be offered
the possibility of redemption. He accepts Tom Riddle—the future
Lord Voldemort—as a Hogwarts student despite his already black-
ened soul; he persuades the Hogwarts headmaster to make Hagrid
gamekeeper after Riddle frames him and Hagrid is expelled from
school; he clings to the innocence of Sirius Black when everyone
else believes him to the Dark Lord's right hand and helps Harry
and Hermione to save Sirius' life; he even allows the Death Eater
Severus Snape—the man who passed Sibyll Trelawney's prophecy to
the Dark Lord and got Harry's parents killed—the opportunity to
become a force for good, a grace that ultimately leads to Snape's
redemption.

Dumbledore is a good man—a "great man," as Hagrid would
always have it—but he is much more than simply this. Lest we
sentimentalize Dumbledore—or worse, sentimentalize God—it's
important to recognize that this love and mercy and unwarranted
grace are also part of a larger package that includes unbelievable
power. Dumbledore is the greatest wizard of his age, a power

119

beyond any other. At the close of *Goblet of Fire*, when Dumbledore rescues Harry from Barty Crouch Jr. in his disguise as Mad-Eye Moody, Harry has an important realization:

> At that moment, Harry fully understood for the first time why people said Dumbledore was the only wizard Voldemort had ever feared. The look upon Dumbledore's face as he stared down at the unconscious form of Mad-Eye Moody was more terrible than Harry could have ever imagined. There was no benign smile upon Dumbledore's face, no twinkle in the eyes behind the spectacles. There was cold fury in every line of the ancient face; a sense of power radiated from Dumbledore as though he were giving off burning heat.[48]

Dumbledore is indeed a great man, kind, loving, a giver of second chances. But he is also powerful, terrible, awesome in the truest sense of the word: inspiring awe (that is, great admiration, amazement, even terror). And this is, as well, our understanding of God the Father, for while we experience and venerate God as a God of love and mercy, God is also the Creator of the world, Being behind all being, a God of power and might, the One to whom the Book of Jude ascribes "glory, majesty, power, and authority" (Jude 25, NRSV). These two qualities—great power and matchless mercy— exist simultaneously in God the Father, as in Dumbledore.

While Albus Dumbledore can teach us about the Christian understanding of God the Father, he also illustrates some of the qualities of God the Son, Jesus Christ. As we have seen, Christians understand Jesus to be the manifestation of God's love in the world; Rowan Williams remarks that we understand this God of love and second chances to be "at work without interruption in the life and work of Jesus . . . it is God who is doing what Jesus is doing," and N. T. Wright suggests that Jesus embodied God's passion for justice, and "that what he did, and what happened to him, set in motion the Creator's plan to rescue the world and put it back to rights."[49] Through Jesus, what is supposed to be righted in the universe is put back on track, despite the best efforts of evil human beings to seize for themselves what should not belong to them. And in Dumbledore we see, like Jesus, an earthly champion

120

of peace and justice, the opposing light to Voldemort's darkness, a force of love and tolerance—and (like Harry) an individual willing to sacrifice for the salvation of others.

In *Order of the Phoenix*, when Dolores Umbridge and her trusted students have recovered the membership list of Dumbledore's Army from the Room of Requirement and captured Harry, who is certain, with the others on the list, to be expelled, Dumbledore weaves a story that allows him to accept all the blame, offering himself up in order to protect Harry and the others:

> "Well, the game is up," [Dumbledore] said simply. "Would you like a written confession from me, Cornelius—or will a statement before these witnesses suffice?" . . .
> "Statement?" said Fudge slowly. "What—I don't—?"
> "Dumbledore's Army, Cornelius," said Dumbledore, still smiling as he waved the list of names before Fudge's face. "Not Potter's Army. *Dumbledore's Army*." . . .
> "Then you have been plotting against me!" [Fudge] yelled.
> "That's right," said Dumbledore cheerfully. . . .
> "Well, well, well—I came here tonight expecting to expel Potter and instead—"
> "Instead you get to arrest me," said Dumbledore, smiling. "It's like losing a Knut and finding a Galleon, isn't it?"[50]

Of course, it is Harry and his fellow members of Dumbledore's Army who have violated school rules and Ministry ordinances; it is they who are guilty, and Dumbledore who is innocent, but as in the Christian narrative, Dumbledore, who is innocent, willingly takes on their guilt to set them free. In this instance of sacrifice in *Order of the Phoenix*, Dumbledore symbolically gives up his life (his identity as Hogwarts' headmaster and teacher) to save those he loves; he also, symbolically, escapes that death by rising to the heavens, rescued by his phoenix, Fawkes. (The phoenix, incidentally, with its power to heal and to rise from the dead, is an ancient emblem of Christianity, and Order of the Phoenix, the community that forms around this ancient Christian symbol of resurrection, is another sign of Rowling's Christian sensibility.)

121

Dumbledore's greatest surrender, of course, comes in his actual sacrificial death at the close of *Half-Blood Prince*. One of the major plotlines running through that novel is Draco Malfoy's commission to kill Dumbledore on Voldemort's orders. Voldemort expects him to fail and for Severus Snape to pick up the pieces; Dumbledore asks Snape to be prepared to kill him before Draco can manage the deed. Dumbledore is concerned, first for innocent bystanders, he says, but he is concerned most explicitly for Draco himself. When Snape asks why, if he is willing to die, he is unwilling to let Draco be the agent of his death instead of himself, Dumbledore says, "That boy's soul is not yet so damaged . . . I would not have it ripped apart on my account."[51] In this, he sounds very much like the Jesus of the crucifixion, who was able to forgive even those who wished his death. Like Jesus, Dumbledore goes willingly to that death, offering his life for a greater good, and like Jesus, Dumbledore also—at least in narrative terms—experiences a resurrection, since Dumbledore greets Harry in the spectral King's Cross Station and blesses him from his Wizarding portrait in the headmaster's office at Hogwarts.

122   Lastly, Dumbledore can provide dramatic exposition of the nature of the final person of the Trinity, the Holy Spirit, which is fortunate, since understandings of the Spirit can be hard to come by in Christian life. The creeds, which are comparatively long-winded on both Father and Son, say that the Holy Spirit is the lord and giver of life, although this doesn't provide a great deal of illumination. In the gospels, the Spirit is described as comforter and advocate, while theologians suggest that the Holy Spirit is the power of God moving in us and uniting us to God and to all those who take up God's holy work on earth. N. T. Wright describes the Spirit as a presence "leading, guiding, warning, rebuking, grieving over our failings, and celebrating our small steps toward the true inheritance."[52] This Spirit is more than conscience, more than comforter; Rowan Williams describes the Holy Spirit as the force moving us toward "Christlikeness."[53]

In all these descriptions we might also see Dumbledore, who is helping Harry become a person willing to be Christ-like, who over and over again serves as Harry's advocate, comforter, and source of wisdom. This last is of some importance; the early church understood the Spirit to be the giver of wisdom, particularly where things were not of the world but spiritual. Consider the end of each novel, where we discover Dumbledore helping Harry and others to make sense not simply of worldly things, but of the spiritual as well. At the end of Harry's first adventure, Dumbledore introduces the idea that death is not so horrifying, as well as the insight that, at least without spiritual guidance, "humans do have a knack of choosing precisely those things that are worst for them."[54] After Harry has entered the Chamber of Secrets, saved Ginny, and destroyed Tom Riddle's diary, Dumbledore helps Harry understand that although Voldemort may have left a bit of himself inside Harry at his dissolution, Harry's soul remains his own to command: "It is our choices, Harry that show what we truly are."[55] And so it continues throughout the series, until in Book 7, after Harry's death (and Dumbledore's), they meet in the nebulous King's Cross Station, and Dumbledore enlightens Harry about Hallows and Horcruxes and Harry's own choices in this life after death—wisdom that again allows Harry to choose what is right over what is easy.

123

In all of these encounters, Dumbledore is both giving Harry soul-wisdom and making it possible for him to become Christ-like, to develop the qualities of spirit that are necessary to save the world. In King's Cross, Dumbledore imparts the final and most important wisdom he ever gives Harry, who wonders if he has to return to earth: "Do not pity the dead, Harry. Pity the living, and, above all, those who live without love. By returning, you may ensure that fewer souls are maimed, fewer families torn apart. If that seems to you a worthy goal, then we say good-bye for the present."[56] After Harry defeats Voldemort, he climbs to the headmaster's office to visit the portrait of Dumbledore, and there he sees Dumbledore weeping with joy, "and the pride and the gratitude emanating from him filled Harry with the same balm as phoenix song," holy and healing music indeed.[57]

Comforter, giver of wisdom, force impelling us to become Christ-like—these are functions of the Holy Spirit. But Christians have long believed that another major function of the Spirit involves gathering the community of God (*ecclesia* in Greek). The Second Letter to the Corinthians opens with a Trinitarian greeting that suggests this work of the Spirit: "The grace of the Lord Jesus Christ, the love of God, and the communion of the Holy Spirit be with all of you" (2 Cor 1:1, NRSV). From Augustine and Aquinas to the modern age, the Spirit has been regarded as the soul or the heart of the church, the bond of love drawing an *ecclesia* together in support and for mission, and in the books, this seems to be Dumbledore's role as well.

We know that Dumbledore was the driving force behind the first Order of the Phoenix ("It's a secret society," Hermione explains to Harry, "Dumbledore's in charge, he founded it"), and we actually get to observe the formation of the second Order.[58] After Cornelius Fudge refuses to take seriously the threat of Voldemort's return at the end of *Goblet of Fire*, Dumbledore moves immediately to gather the forces of light and love in opposition to the powers of death and hatred: "There is work to be done. . . . Molly . . . am I right in thinking that I can count on you and Arthur? . . . Then I need to send a message to Arthur," said Dumbledore. "All those that we can persuade of the truth must be notified immediately."[59] Dumbledore sends Hagrid to parley with the giants and Sirius to alert "the old crowd," and we watch as the Order of the Phoenix takes shape before our very eyes—thanks to Dumbledore's guidance and inspiration.[60]

The World to Come

The point of community and moral formation, as Rowling suggested in her discussion of the creation of Hogwarts, is a world in which one's differences do not separate people in and of themselves but are seen instead as a vital part of creation. Tertullian wrote that while Christians called themselves brother and sister, they also claimed kinship with all human beings.[61] This movement toward harmony is ultimately where we end up in the Potter stories, with even the offensive Slytherin gathered into kinship—or at least some of them. Christians understand that when they assemble with diverse others as a church (what in Greek is called an *ecclesia*), they are participating in more than just a remaking of ourselves; they are participating in God's plan for the world. When the *ecclesia* does its work, it is participating in a faithful understanding that someday we will no longer be alienated or separated from ourselves, others, or God by evil and death; someday, death itself will die.

In the course of J. K. Rowling's epic story, we follow Harry through adventure after adventure. Characters live and die—and live again. Evil is everywhere—and then evil is defeated. But what Rowling has written about in Harry Potter's story is not simply a story about defeating an evil, but about planting great good, not simply about an individual's resurrection, but about a world's renewal—a story about making all things new, if you will. The ending of *Deathly Hallows* (and Harry's story) is a powerful eucatastrophe: Truth is exposed, joy and sorrow are reconciled at the moment of greatest crisis, and, at this moment, some vision of the "Great World" beyond the story is revealed.[62] Of all Rowling's reflections of Christian belief, perhaps this is the most important: out of great suffering comes great good, and that good is for more than just a single individual.

When Rowling has talked about the seventh book and its ending, she has noted that Harry's victory over Voldemort—the symbolic victory of love over death—has had tangible consequences for more than just Harry, who was returned to life. As she describes the world that followed that victory, she has talked about how "the Ministry of Magic was de-corrupted, and with Kingsley [Shacklebolt] at the helm the discrimination that was always latent there was eradicated. Harry, Ron, Hermione, Ginny, et al. would of course play a significant part in the re-building of wizarding society through their future careers." The world itself, post-Voldemort, even looks brighter and more beautiful; Rowling said that with the Dementors banished, even foggy Britain enjoys a new spray of sunshine.[63]

The world that follows the Second Wizarding War is a world into which the king has returned (Kingley's name, wonderfully, contains both suggestions of royalty and the breaking of shackles; in familiar religious terms, he is the king who frees the people from bondage), a world that has been altered by a cataclysmic event—the end of the world, seemingly—into a place of greater love, compassion,

125

kindness, and beauty. While still obviously an imperfect world (for Harry becomes an auror, trained to hunt down dark wizards, and Hermione works in magical law enforcement, which implies continuing disagreement and conflict), this world that follows Harry's resurrection can stand in for that perfect world to come in secular and Christian understandings of the end of things. It is a new world, marvelously and even miraculously changed from the dark world threatened in the darkest days of Voldemort's ascendancy. Death has been defeated—if not permanently, as the gospel account predicts—and a new reign of justice has begun.

The inscription on the Potters' grave tells us that the last enemy to be defeated is death—and Christianity has certainly seemed very interested in the question of what happens to our souls after death. Rowling, likewise, is drawn to exploration of this mystery. As we saw earlier, she spotlighted the verse from First Corinthians as a thematic center for the entire series, created an ultimate villain who tries to create his own dark brand of immortality instead of trusting to anything outside himself, and in a post-*Hallows* interview has confessed that she wrestles with the question of belief in an eternal soul: "On any given moment if you asked me if I believed in life after death . . . I think I would come down on the side of yes . . . But it's something that I wrestle with a lot. It preoccupies me a lot, and I think that's very obvious within the books."[64] The concern with living well, with confronting death, and with belief in a better future drives the good characters in Potter—and perhaps Rowling herself—and the Christian belief that death is not the end and evil does not have the final word does stand as a huge consolation in the face of darkness.

For many Christians this is at the core of their beliefs, and Rowling's admission that this is one of the central elements of faith with which she struggles is certainly not unusual. Religion has always been a way to impose some meaning on the chaos of life, to assert that our little lives do not mark the full extent of our experience in the cosmos. But Christianity is not *merely* about defeating death; the new life that follows transformation is not just about life for the individual, but life for the world. When Christians recite the historic Nicene Creed, the phrase with which they conclude goes like this: "We look for the resurrection of the dead, and the life of the world to come." The resurrection of the dead and the life of the world to come are inextricably linked; as Jürgen Moltmann reminds us, there can be no resurrection of the dead until the new earth arrives in which death will die.[65] In the world to come, death will no longer hold power over us, which should give us great comfort and joy, but more importantly, in this world what *was* has been transformed as well, and this transformation of the world is what underlies all the other beautiful changes to come, including the end of death.

However Rowling personally may struggle with the question of life after death in her personal faith, she has come down on the side of life in her fiction, and many others—Christians and non-Christians alike—also believe that death is not the ultimate end of our selves. As we see how the Harry Potter story deals with these hopes of life after death and the life of the world to come, we can see how the saga reflects familiar stories and beliefs about death and immortality. But because even devout Christians display a wide range of beliefs about what immortality might mean—N. T. Wright argues that most people don't really know what orthodox Christian belief actually is; out of their tangle of beliefs, they mostly have a vague and fuzzy optimism that somehow things will work out in the end—so it may be instructive to discover what we might learn about Christian belief (unorthodox and orthodox alike) through Rowling's apocalyptic ending to the Harry Potter saga—and our visions of the new world that follows.[66]

Although Rowling returns again and again to the themes of mortality and immortality, some skeptics might argue that there is little we can learn about Christian belief in the afterlife from the epic, citing her widely diverse examples of what we might call life after death—the Hogwarts ghosts and Peeves the Poltergeist, the "living" portraits of dead Hogwarts headmasters, the veil in the Department of Mysteries, and, of course, the scene in the King's Cross Station in which Harry—not, on the whole, dead—meets a Dumbledore who is assuredly so. We learn in the Potter books

127

about Dementors, who do not kill the physical body, but somehow can steal a person's immortal soul, leaving behind nothing but that body. We also discover various magical means for cheating death and achieving immortality, such as Nicolas Flamel's Elixir of Life and Voldemort's Horcruxes.

Still, even with these multifold examples, I think we can discern a common pattern in Rowling's references to death and life after death: these story elements all suggest that there must be some sort of existence that survives our physical death. Sometimes Rowling is more explicit: at the climax of the *Deathly Hallows*, we read that when Harry uses the Resurrection Stone, "It did not matter about bringing [his parents] back, for he was about to join them. He was not really fetching them: They were fetching him."[67] Harry believes that his soul will survive his encounter with Voldemort, even if his physical body does not. At the end of *The Order of the Phoenix*, Harry imagines Sirius on the other side of the veil, and when possessed by Voldemort and in agony, he thinks, "*Let him kill us. . . . End it, Dumbledore. . . . Death is nothing compared to this. . . . And I'll see Sirius again.*"[68] And Dumbledore, in his commentary to *Beedle the Bard*, writes that: "While we have devised innumerable ways of maintaining the illusion of our loved ones' continuing presence [Dumbledore notes the example of Wizarding photos and portraits that move and even talk like their subjects], wizards still have not found a way of reuniting body and soul once death has occurred."[69] All of these examples (and others) postulate a life after physical death—and a soul that separates from the body at death to continue on its journey.

128

In this notion of the divisibility of body and soul, Harry and Dumbledore (and Rowling) are restating a belief popularized by Plato and still held by many people, including many devout Christians: the fundamental—if not fundamentally orthodox— understanding of the separation of the immortal soul from the temporal body. Christians often testify that they believe in life after death, that their souls will continue after their bodies die, and that their existence is ongoing. They think of this as life after death. But as Wright observes, to believe that we will continue on as disembodied souls is actually to give death the final victory: "If the promised final future is simply that immortal souls leave behind their mortal bodies, then death still rules—since that is a description not of the *defeat* of death but simply of death itself."[70] How can we speak of the last enemy, death, being defeated, if the effects of death continue?

Actual bodily resurrection—despite the biblical narrative of Jesus' resurrection—can be a challenge for many people. Yet bodily resurrection is the orthodox Christian belief, and both Wright's and Moltmann's theological restatements of resurrection are drawn from the teachings of the Apostle Paul and from the classic creedal statements of Christianity that "We believe in the resurrection of the body." As in the example of Harry, who returns bodily to the world after his death, or like the post-resurrection accounts of Jesus, whose resurrected body was clearly a physical body that could eat, speak, and be touched (if also different from the body Jesus had possessed before his death), orthodox Christian belief is that God will resurrect all believers as God raised Jesus, in physical forms, not through the eternal survival of a bodiless soul.

129

We believe in the resurrection of the body. True Christian belief is not about the immortality of souls; it is about the impossibility of separating bodies and souls. This is why the Dementor's kiss seems so horrifying—and blasphemous. (How dare they—how can anything—presume to destroy the soul?) When the Ministry sends Dementors to perform the kiss on Sirius Black, Dumbledore speaks of how "Sirius will be worse than dead."[71] When Harry speaks about saving Dudley from the Dementors, he rightly points out at their final goodbye that he was not saving Dudley's life: he was preserving his soul. And when Barty Crouch Jr. is destroyed by the Dementors—even a fiend such as he—Harry, Professor McGonagall, and others are appalled by the act.

But just as the thought of a body without a soul is wrong, so is the belief of a soul without a body; to insist on the physicality of resurrection is to insist on more than Christian orthodoxy. As we saw in chapter 1, the Gnostic heresy suggested that the physical world is inferior to the spiritual world, and if we believe that this life and the bodies we occupy are ultimately unimportant—that we will all "go to heaven" and leave the physical behind—then that belief will have powerful implications for the way we think and act in this world.

J. K Rowling closed her epic with the words "All was well," but she didn't set those words in some far-distant heaven; the final chapter of *Deathly Hallows* takes place on Earth, at King's Cross Station, in the midst of our own physical reality. Rowling's apocalyptic battle has been fought—and won, because of Harry's sacrifice, resurrection, and physical return—and the world that follows is changed as a result. And this final lesson tells us something about Christian belief—even if, again, it is something that many Christians do not know they believe.

"I believe in the Kingdom Come," U2's lead singer Bono sings, in an elliptical take on the Christian statement familiar to us from the so-called Lord's Prayer, the prayer Jesus told his followers that they were to use when they wanted to approach the divine. In that prayer, we are reminded that what we are praying—and working—toward is not some distant heaven, but a transformation of Earth: "Our Father in heaven, may your name be held holy, your kingdom come, your will be done, on earth as in heaven" (Matt 6:9b-10, NJB). As N. T. Wright observed, "the prayer was powerfully answered at the first Easter and will finally be answered fully when heaven and earth are joined in the new Jerusalem."[72] The resurrection of Jesus—and the resurrection of Harry in his story—kicks off the transformation of the world that marks the golden future, a future of justice, peace, love, and compassion, that will ultimately transform our world—not some distant heavenly city—into an earthly paradise.

What Bishop Wright argues—that "the world to come" will be this world, transformed by the miraculous power of God and marked by the resurrection of Jesus Christ—is his conclusion after analyzing the biblical record and the narrative of God's justice and mercy. While Wright is one of our greatest contemporary scholars, his conclusion does stand in contrast to the beliefs of many

Christians expecting a heaven with streets paved with gold and a martially wondrous second coming of Jesus; yet it is so perfectly illustrated by Harry Potter's story that we can see the power and beauty of the theory.

Harry's new world fits as well with a common secular belief—the belief in progress—that many who do not explicitly share Christian belief nonetheless have taken as their own future hope. John Gray notes that this belief in a movement toward a more perfect world, a staple of Western thought since the Enlightenment, is strongly shaped by Christian belief in a future in which sickness, death, famine, hunger, war, and oppression will end after a climactic battle in which the forces of evil will be completely destroyed. These secular dreams for a brand new world on the far side of conflict are, Gray argues, actually "spilt theology."[73]

But as Gray and many others point out, the secular myth of hope and progress has run headlong into the realities of human nature. Over the centuries, many groups and societies have aimed at perfection—and missed by a mile. The Wizarding community, populated by men and women devoted to knowledge and self-control, nonetheless employs foul methods in pursuit of its better future: Dementors guard prisoners in Azkaban; Ministry officials give preference to those with the deepest pockets; and some, like Barty Crouch Sr. and Dolores Umbridge, even use the ruthless methods of the enemy to try and protect against what they perceive as the enemy. These failures are not merely in Harry's story; even the United States of America, founded in pursuit of noble dreams like religious and political freedom, and mythologized by Americans and others as a promised land, has slaughtered indigenous peoples, enslaved Africans, and, more recently, held prisoners incommunicado in our own inaccessible Azkabans. Those who believe in America—and I count myself among them—have always worked to remind it of its core beliefs, but history suggests that our best intentions will not necessarily yield a brave new world.

Something larger than us and our intentions may be necessary.

Indeed, the apocalyptic ending to Harry's story reminds us that

131

our belief in a better world to come does require our participation and assent, but it also requires something beyond ourselves—a miracle of some sort. In Harry's case, courageous battle and ingenious defenses are not enough to defeat Voldemort and launch a new way of living; in fact, Harry's story tells us that instead of courageous battle, courageous faith is what is required. Harry doesn't have—and never has had—a chance against Voldemort, fighting wizard to wizard. What he has instead of the way of the warrior is the way of surrender, a faith in something larger and more powerful than himself, a belief in a force of justice that will bring everything right, somehow—even death—so that those Harry loves will not have to be afraid any more. There must be—and is—in the mythology of C. S. Lewis' Narnia, some Deeper Magic that underlies all we see. And after the miraculous events of Harry's willing death out of love—and resurrection—the world can move past cataclysmic violence and wrenching despair and toward a beautiful future.

Thus the conclusion of *Deathly Hallows* presents the Christian hope in brief, is emblematic of the miraculous new earthly kingdom that follows the sacred death and return. The Apostle Paul spoke of Jesus as the first citizen of the new kingdom, and recorded the great early poem of the church:

> He is the Head of the Body, that is, the Church.
> He is the Beginning, the first-born from the dead, so that he
> should be supreme in every way;
> because God wanted all fullness to be found in him
> and through him to reconcile all things to him,
> everything in heaven and everything on earth,
> by making peace through his death on the cross.
> You were once estranged and of hostile intent through your evil
> behaviour;
> now he has reconciled you, by his death and in that mortal
> body,
> to bring you before himself holy, faultless and irreproachable—
> (Col 1:18-22, NJB)

Just as Jesus is first born of the new creation, so is Harry the first to encounter the victory of love over death; Harry, we might

132

say, is the first citizen of his new world, the first sign of what is possible. In the end of *Deathly Hallows* and Rowling's glimpses into the world that follows, we might also say that we are reading a powerful narrative about our own hope for the future.

What happens may not be up to us, but we are called to participate in what is coming. Harry, Ron, Hermione, Dumbledore, and the Order of the Phoenix did not all reach that future, but all of them worked toward a world of love, compassion, acceptance, and justice, a world that, as Remus Lupin told Harry, he would hope to bequeath to his son. When Hermione spoke out against prejudice or stood bravely and patiently in the face of it; when Ron gulped away his fear and did what he knew was right; when Dumbledore devoted his life to providing second chances, working for equality, and asserting our common humanity; when, out of love, Lily Potter gave her life trying to protect the child she had brought into the world; and when Harry, out of love, gave his life because he knew it was the only way to save those he loved—all of these (and many more) were working for the coming of Kingsley's kingdom, even though they did not know it. When Lupin spoke on *Potter-watch* during the darkest of times, he reminded his listeners that Harry Potter represented everything for which they were fighting, everything that truly mattered: good over evil, innocence, and the need to continue in the face of difficulty.[74] They were working for the kingdom, believing that it would come someday, even if they couldn't see how it might come.

And then, at last, miraculously, it did.

We too are called to work for the coming of that earthly paradise, that world in which the lion and lamb (or the Gryffindor and Slytherin) will lie down together, that time when war, disease, and destruction will just be words. In Christian belief, the fate of the world does lie in God's hands; so does the fate of our souls. But we are directed to actively participate in what is coming as a sign of what is coming. Grace, love, and miraculous events change the world—but so too does our voluntary participation in that change. When we respond to that call with courage, faith, and love, as the Order did, we throw our talents and our lives behind what really matters. When we live our lives in love, as Lily and Harry did, we are participating in the Deeper Magic of the universe, the love of a creator for its creation.

The end of the world is always coming, and disaster is always looming; this is the nature of the world we inhabit. But over six hundred years ago, the medieval mystic Julian of Norwich had a series of visions in which God spoke to her about sin, death, and life, and in the passage best remembered today, assured her that however bad things looked at the moment, there was an order, justice, and truth operating in the universe: "All shall be well, and all shall be well, and all manner of thing shall be well."

And this is the promise of the Deeper Magic, of a world where love can never be defeated by death.

In the end, the end of the world is not to be feared, but welcomed, a new birth instead of a final death. And if, like Harry, we too live faithfully and in hope, our stories tell us that someday we too will live in a world where all is well.

Notes

Introduction

1 The first Harry Potter novel bears this name in its native England and elsewhere, although it was retitled *Harry Potter and the Sorcerer's Stone* for its American publication. I will henceforth use *Sorcerer's Stone* to cite the American edition of the book, but *Philosophers' Stone* in discussion.

2 Jules Bearman, personal email, June 2, 2009.

3 Nancy Gibbs, "The Moment, 7/14/09: Peoria, Ill.," *Time*, August 3, 2009, 13.

4 Dinitia Smith, "The Times Plans a Children's Best-Seller List," *The New York Times*, June 24, 2000, http://www.nytimes.com/2000/06/24/books/the-times-plans-a-children-s-best-seller-list.html.

5 Julie Watson and Tomas Kellner, "J. K. Rowling and The Billion-Dollar Empire," *Forbes*, February 26, 2004, http://www.forbes.com/2004/02/26/cx_jw_0226rowlingbill04.html.

6 Reuters, "New Harry Potter Movie Sets World Opening Record," *Yahoo! News*, July 16, 2009, http://news.yahoo.com/; Pamela McClintock, "'Harry Potter' Pulls in $22.2 Million," *Variety*, July 15, 2009, http://www.variety.com/article/VR1118006002.html?categoryid=1082&cs=1.

7 Dave McNary, "Warner Bros. Stocks Tentpole Closet," *Variety*, July 11, 2009, http://www.variety.com/article/VR1118005884.html?categoryid=13&cs=1.

8   Tomas Kellner, "Harry Potter and the Billion-Dollar Brand," *Forbes*, March 13, 2005, http://www.forbes.com/2005/03/10/cz_tk_0310potter _bill05.html?boxes=custom.

9   http://harrypotterfanfiction.com (accessed June 15, 2007).

10   Lev Grossman, "The Boy Who Rocked," *Time*, July 20, 2009, 63.

11   C. S. Lewis, *An Experiment in Criticism* (Cambridge: University of Cambridge Press, 1965), 2; C. S. Lewis, "On Stories," in *Essays Presented to Charles Williams*, ed. C. S. Lewis (1947; Grand Rapids: Eerdmans, 1966), 92–93, 102.

12   Lewis, "On Stories," 103, 105.

13   J. K. Rowling, *Harry Potter and the Deathly Hallows* (New York: Scholastic, 2007), 125–26 (here and throughout this book all emphasis is in the original); Lewis, *An Experiment in Criticism*, 137.

14   Lewis, *An Experiment in Criticism*, 85; Northrop Frye, "Reconsidering Levels of Meaning," *Christianity and Literature* 54 (2005): 417.

Chapter 1

1   Nancy Gibbs, "J. K. Rowling," *Time*, December 19, 2007, http:// www.time.com/time/specials/2007/personoftheyear/article/0,28804 ,1690753_1695388_1695436,00.html.

2   The original e-mail was archived at *Urban Legends*,http://urbanlegends .about.com/library/weekly/aa080900b.htm.

3   *The Onion* article "*Harry Potter* Books Spark Rise In Satanism Among Children" was quoted in both the email and as a source in online postings against the books. *The Onion*, July 26, 2000, http://www .theonion.com/content/news/harry_potter_books_spark_rise_in.

4   "Pope's Top Exorcist Says Harry Potter Is 'King of Darkness,'" *CBC News*, September 3, 2006, http://www.cbc.ca/arts/story/2006/09/03/ harrypotter-exorcist-pope.html.

5   "Harry Potter Is 'The Wrong Kind of Hero' According to the Vatican," *Daily Mail*, January 15, 2008, http://www.dailymail.co.uk/ news/article-508369/Harry-Potter-wrong-kind-hero-according -Vatican.html.

6   "Emirates Ban Harry Potter Book," *BBC News*, February 12, 2002, http://news.bbc.co.uk/2/hi/entertainment/1816012.stm.

7   Nick Squires, "Harry Potter and the Half-Blood Prince Praised by Vatican," *The Telegraph*, July 14, 2009, http://www.telegraph.co.uk/ culture/film/film-news/5826251/Harry-Potter-and-the-Half-Blood -Prince-praised-by-Vatican.html.

8   "Dr. Dobson: What I Think about *Harry Potter*," *Focus on the Family*, http://listen.family.org/miscdaily/A000000593.cfm.

9   "JK Rowling under Fire from US Bible Belt after Outing Dumbledore

as Gay," *Daily Mail*, October 28, 2007, http://www.dailymail.co.uk/news/article-490261/JK-Rowling-US-Bible-belt-outing-Dumbledore-gay.html#.

10 Melissa Anelli, *Harry, A History* (New York: Pocket, 2008), 196.

11 "Harry Potter Tops List of Most Challenged Books of 21st Century," *American Library Association*, September 21, 2006, http://www.ala.org/Template.cfm?Section=News&template=/ContentManagement/ContentDisplay.cfm&ContentID=138540.

12 *The Today Show*, NBC, October 20, 2000. Interview transcribed at http://www.accio-quote.org/articles/2000/1000-nbc-couric.htm.

13 J. K. Rowling, *Harry Potter and the Sorcerer's Stone* (New York: Scholastic, 1998), 1.

14 Rowling, *Sorcerer's Stone*, 4.

15 Rowling, *Sorcerer's Stone*, 15.

16 Jeff Jensen, "'Fire' Storm," *Entertainment Weekly*, September 7, 2000, http://www.ew.com/ew/article/0,,85523,00.html.

17 Rowling, *Sorcerer's Stone*, 65.

18 Alister E. McGrath, *Christian Theology: An Introduction*, 4th ed. (Malden, Mass.: Blackwell, 2007), 225.

19 J. K. Rowling, *Harry Potter and the Goblet of Fire* (New York: Scholastic, 2000), 15.

20 J. K. Rowling, *Harry Potter and the Deathly Hallows* (New York: Scholastic, 2007), 440.

21 "J. K. Rowling at the Royal Albert Hall, 26 June 2003," *Accio Quote!* http://www.accio-quote.org/articles/2003/0626-alberthall-fry.htm.

22 Rowling, *Sorcerer's Stone*, 13.

23 Rowling, *Sorcerer's Stone*, 77.

24 J. K. Rowling, *Harry Potter and the Chamber of Secrets* (New York: Scholastic, 1999), 51.

25 Rowling, *Sorcerer's Stone*, 78.

26 "J. K. Rowling at the Royal Albert Hall," *Accio Quote!*

27 Rowling, *Chamber of Secrets*, 115–16.

28 J. K. Rowling, *The Tales of Beedle the Bard* (New York: Scholastic, 2008), 41.

29 J. K. Rowling, *Harry Potter and the Half-Blood Prince* (New York: Scholastic, 2005), 4.

30 Rowling, *Half-Blood Prince*, 18.

31 Rowling, *Chamber of Secrets*, 43.

32 Rowling, *Deathly Hallows*, 37.

33 J. K. Rowling, *Harry Potter and the Prisoner of Azkaban* (New York: Scholastic, 1999), 38.

34 J. R. R. Tolkien, *The Letters of J. R. R. Tolkien*, ed. Humphrey Carpenter (1981; Boston: Houghton Mifflin, 2000), 145–46.

35 Rowling, *Deathly Hallows*, 9.

36 Martin Luther King Jr., "Our God Is Able," in *Strength to Love* (Philadelphia: Fortress, 1963), 107.

37 Rowling, *The Tales of Beedle the Bard*, 107.

38 Rowling, *Sorcerer's Stone*, 118.

39 Rowling, *Half-Blood Prince*, 273.

40 Rowling, *Goblet of Fire*, 217.

41 Rowling, *Goblet of Fire*, 213.

42 Rowling, *Goblet of Fire*, 213.

43 Rowling, *Goblet of Fire*, 217.

44 J. K. Rowling, *Harry Potter and the Order of the Phoenix* (New York: Scholastic, 2003), 810.

45 Rowling, *Half-Blood Prince*, 522–23.

46 Rowling, *Half-Blood Prince*, 531.

47 J. R. R. Tolkien, "On Fairy-Stories," in *Tales from the Perilous Realm* (Boston: Houghton Mifflin, 2008), 152.

48 Lisa Miller, "BeliefWatch: Christ-Like," *Newsweek*, http://www.newsweek.com/id/32595.

49 C. S. Lewis, "Sometimes Fairy Stories May Say Best What's to Be Said," *Of Other Worlds: Essays and Stories*, ed. Walter Hooper (New York: Harcourt Brace & Jovanovich, 1966), 37.

50 Karen Armstrong, *The Battle for God: A History of Fundamentalism* (New York: Ballantine, 2000), xv–xvi.

51 George MacDonald, *A Dish of Orts*, 1893 (Whitefish, Mt.: Kessinger, 2004), 9.

52 C. S. Lewis, "The Dethronement of Power," *Time and Tide* 36 (October 22, 1955): 1374.

53 Stanley Hauerwas, *A Community of Character: Toward a Constructive Christian Social Ethic* (Notre Dame: University of Notre Dame Press, 1982), 148.

54 Ralph C. Wood, *The Gospel According to Tolkien: Visions of the Kingdom in Middle-Earth* (Louisville: Westminster John Knox, 2003), 1.

55 Tolkien, *The Letters of J. R. R. Tolkien*, 326.

56 Rowling has pointed out on many occasions that within the first pages of *Harry Potter and the Philosopher's Stone* we learn of the brutal murder of Harry's parents. Death and loss infuse the entire series, although we do not directly witness deaths of characters who matter to us until *Harry Potter and the Goblet of Fire*, four books into the series.

57 Rowling, *The Tales of Beedle the Bard*, 17, 19.

58 Tolkien, "On Fairy-Stories," 381, 383.
59 "J. K. Rowling Web Chat Transcript," *The Leaky Cauldron*, July 30, 2007, http://www.the-leaky-cauldron.org/2007/7/30/j-k-rowling-web -chat-transcript.
60 Tolkien, "On Fairy-Stories," 384.

Chapter 2

1 J. K. Rowling, *Harry Potter and the Sorcerer's Stone* (New York: Scholastic, 1998), 34.
2 Rowling, *Sorcerer's Stone*, 30.
3 Alan Jacobs, "Harry Potter's Magic," *First Things* 99 (January 2000): 35–38, http://www.firstthings.com/article/2007/01/harry-potters-magic -28.
4 "J. K. Rowling at the Royal Albert Hall, 26 June 2003," *Accio Quote!* http://www.accio-quote.org/articles/2003/0626-alberthall-fry.htm.
5 Charles Kimball, *When Religion Becomes Evil* (New York: Harper-SanFrancisco, 2002), 39.
6 J. K. Rowling, *Harry Potter and the Order of the Phoenix* (New York: Scholastic, 2003), 66.
7 J. K. Rowling, *Harry Potter and the Goblet of Fire* (New York: Scholastic, 2000), 214–15.
8 Rowling, *Goblet of Fire*, 218.
9 J. K. Rowling, *Harry Potter and the Deathly Hallows* (New York: Scholastic, 2007), 198.
10 J. K. Rowling, "The Fringe Benefits of Failure, and the Importance of Imagination," *Harvard Magazine*, June 5, 2008, http://harvard magazine.com/commencement/the-fringe-benefits-failure-the -importance-imagination.
11 "Rowling Answers 10 Questions About Harry," *Time*, http://www.time .com/time/specials/2007/personoftheyear/article/0,28804,1690753 _1695388_1695569,00.html.
12 Rowling, *Deathly Hallows*, 741.
13 Rowling, *Order of the Phoenix*, 824.
14 Rowling, *Order of the Phoenix*, 855–56.
15 C. S. Lewis, *The Great Divorce* (New York: Macmillan, 1946), 19.
16 J. K. Rowling, *Harry Potter and the Half-Blood Prince* (New York: Scholastic, 2005), 78.
17 Rowling, *Order of the Phoenix*, 206.
18 Henri Nouwen, "June 13," in *Bread for the Journey: A Daybook of Wisdom and Faith* (San Francisco: HarperSanFrancisco, 1997), n.p.
19 Rowling, *Half-Blood Prince*, 55.

20   Barbara Brown Taylor, *The Seeds of Heaven: Sermons on the Gospel of Matthew* (Louisville: Westminster John Knox, 2004), 85.
21   J. K. Rowling, *Harry Potter and the Prisoner of Azkaban* (New York: Scholastic, 1999), 2.
22   Rowling, *Sorcerer's Stone*, 213–14.
23   "Rowling Answers 10 Questions About Harry," *Time.*
24   Rowling, *Sorcerer's Stone*, 114.
25   J. K. Rowling, *Harry Potter and the Chamber of Secrets* (New York: Scholastic, 1999), 42.
26   Rowling, *Half-Blood Prince*, 77.
27   Rowling, *Goblet of Fire*, 339.
28   Rowling, *Goblet of Fire*, 177.
29   Melissa Anelli and Emerson Spartz, "The Leaky Cauldron and Mugglenet Interview: Joanne Kathleen Rowling: Part Three," *The Leaky Cauldron*, July 16, 2005, http://www.the-leaky-cauldron.org/features/interviews/jkr3.
30   Anelli and Spartz, "The Leaky Cauldron."
31   Rowling, *Goblet of Fire*, 723.
32   Rowling, *Deathly Hallows*, 610.
33   Rowling, *Deathly Hallows*, 749.
34   Anelli and Spartz, "The Leaky Cauldron."
35   Rowling, *Sorcerer's Stone*, 120.
36   Rowling, *Deathly Hallows*, 745–46.
37   Rowling, *Deathly Hallows*, 756.
38   "J. K. Rowling Web Chat Transcript," *The Leaky Cauldron*, July 30, 2007, http://www.the-leaky-cauldron.org/2007/7/30/j-k-rowling-web-chat-transcript.
39   Rowling, *Deathly Hallows*, 758
40   Rowling, *Goblet of Fire*, 708.
41   Rowling, *Order of the Phoenix*, 340.
42   Rowling, *Order of the Phoenix*, 761.
43   Rowling, *Order of the Phoenix*, 761.
44   Rowling, *Deathly Hallows*, 574.
45   Xenophon, *The Memorabilia*, II.vi.
46   Rowling, *Order of the Phoenix*, 838–39.
47   "J. K. Rowling at the Royal Albert Hall," *Accio Quote!*
48   "J. K. Rowling Web Chat Transcript," *The Leaky Cauldron.*
49   Rowling, *Half-Blood Prince*, 277.

Chapter 3

1   Pete Cashmore, "Michael Jackson Dies: Twitter Tributes Now 30% of Tweets," *Mashable*, June 25, 2009, http://mashable.com/2009/06/25/

michael-jackson-twitter; Pete Cashmore, "Michael Jackson Funeral: 500,000+ Facebook Updates Posted," *Mashable*, July 7, 2009, http://mashable.com/2009/07/07/michael-jackson-funeral-facebook.

2   J. K. Rowling, *Harry Potter and the Sorcerer's Stone* (New York: Scholastic, 1998), 13.

3   Rowling, *Sorcerer's Stone*, 95.

4   J. K. Rowling, *Harry Potter and the Half-Blood Prince* (New York: Scholastic, 2005), 136.

5   J. K. Rowling, *Harry Potter and the Chamber of Secrets* (New York: Scholastic, 1999), 61.

6   Rowling, *Chamber of Secrets*, 297.

7   "J. K. Rowling Web Chat Transcript," *The Leaky Cauldron*, July 30, 2007, http://www.the-leaky-cauldron.org/2007/7/30/j-k-rowling-web-chat-transcript.

8   Rowling, *Sorcerer's Stone*, 108–9.

9   Rowling, *Half-Blood Prince*, 138–39.

10   Rowling, *Half-Blood Prince*, 312.

11   Rowling, *Half-Blood Prince*, 314.

12   Rowling, *Sorcerer's Stone*, 297.

13   Joseph Campbell, *The Hero with a Thousand Faces* (1949; Princeton: Princeton University Press, 1972), 16.

14   Campbell, *Hero*, 38.   141

15   Joseph Campbell with Bill Moyers, *The Power of Myth* (New York: Anchor, 1988), 82.

16   Rowling, *Sorcerer's Stone*, 297.

17   J. K. Rowling, *Harry Potter and the Goblet of Fire* (New York: Scholastic, 2000), ch. 24.

18   Paul Tillich, *Existence and the Christ, Systematic Theology*, vol. 2 (Chicago: University of Chicago Press, 1957), 166.

19   Hendrikus Berkhof, *Christian Faith: An Introduction to the Study of the Faith*, trans. Sierd Woudstra (1973; Grand Rapids: Eerdmans, 1979), 208–9.

20   Rowling, *Goblet of Fire*, 213.

21   "J. K. Rowling Web Chat Transcript," *The Leaky Cauldron*.

22   Rowling, *Goblet of Fire*, 707.

23   Rowling, *Half-Blood Prince*, 14.

24   J. K. Rowling, *Harry Potter and the Order of the Phoenix* (New York: Scholastic, 2003), 267.

25   Rowling, *Order of the Phoenix*, 746.

26   Rowan Williams, "General Synod London Sessions, 15–16 November 2005, Archbishop's Contribution in Debate on Terrorism," http://www.archbishopofcanterbury.org/2259; Peter Oborne, "A Conspiracy That

Is as Foul as It Gets," *Daily Mail,* 7 February 2009, http://www.dailymail
.co.uk/debate/article-1137164/PETER-OBORNE-A-conspiracy-foul
-gets.html.

27   Rowan Williams, *Writing in the Dust: After September 11* (Grand
Rapids: Eerdmans, 2002) 34.

28   J. K. Rowling, *Harry Potter and the Deathly Hallows* (New York:
Scholastic, 2007), 123.

29   J. K. Rowling, *Harry Potter and the Prisoner of Azkaban* (New York:
Scholastic, 1999), 393.

30   Peter J. Gomes, *The Good Book: Reading the Bible with Mind and
Heart* (New York: Morrow), 256.

31   Rowling, *Goblet of Fire,* 239.

32   Rowling, *Goblet of Fire,* 238.

33   J. K. Rowling, "The Fringe Benefits of Failure, and the Importance of Imagination," *Harvard Magazine* June 5, 2008, http://
harvardmagazine.com/commencement/the-fringe-benefits-failure-the
-importance-imagination.

34   Rowling, *Goblet of Fire,* 125.

35   Rowling, *Deathly Hallows,* 103.

36   Rowling, *Goblet of Fire,* 100.

37   Rowling, *Deathly Hallows,* 35.

38   Rowling, *Deathly Hallows,* 40.

39   Rowling, *Deathly Hallows,* 42.

40   "J. K. Rowling Web Chat Transcript," *The Leaky Cauldron.*

41   Rowling, *Deathly Hallows,* 606.

42   Rowling, *Deathly Hallows,* 605–6.

43   "J. K. Rowling Web Chat Transcript," *The Leaky Cauldron.*

44   Rowling, *Deathly Hallows,* 378–79.

45   Rowling, *Deathly Hallows,* 381.

46   Rowling, *Deathly Hallows,* 361.

47   Rowling, *Deathly Hallows,* 361.

142

Chapter 4

1   In 2005 the Rt. Rev. David Lacy, the head of the Church of Scotland,
chose *Harry Potter and the Half-Blood Prince* as his book of the
year, citing the victory of good over evil and respectfully disagreeing
with those Christians who believe the books are "dangerous and anti-
Christian." Maria Mackay, "Church of Scotland Moderator on Harry
Potter," *Christian Today,* December 6, 2005, http://www.christian
today.com/article/church.of.scotland.votes.harry.potter.as.book.of
.the.year/4715.htm.

2   Nancy Gibbs, "J. K. Rowling," *Time,* December 19, 2007, http://
    www.time.com/time/specials/2007/personoftheyear/article/0,28804
    ,1690753_1695388_1695436,00.html.

3   Gibbs, "J. K. Rowling."

4   Alison Lurie, "Not for Muggles," *New York Review of Books,* December 16, 1999, http://www.nybooks.com/articles/264.

5   Bob Smietana, "The Gospel According to J. K. Rowling," *Christianity Today,* July 23, 2007, http://www.christianitytoday.com/ct/2007/julyweb-only/130-12.0.html; Lisa Miller, "BeliefWatch: Christ-Like," *Newsweek,* http://www.newsweek.com/id/32595.

6   Jeffrey Weiss, "Christian Themes Abound in Potter," *Dallas Morning News,* July 29, 2007, http://www.dallasnews.com/sharedcontent/dws/dn/opinion/viewpoints/stories/DN-weiss_28edi.ART.State.Edition1.2758dd6.html.

7   C. S. Lewis, "Christianity and Literature," *The Seeing Eye and Other Selected Essays from* Christian Reflections (1967; New York: Ballantine, 1986), 2.

8   Madeleine L'Engle, *Walking on Water: Reflections on Faith and Art* (1980; New York: North Point Press, 1995), 122.

9   Shawn Adler, "'Harry Potter' Author J. K. Rowling Opens Up About Books' Christian Imagery," MTV.com, October 17, 2007, http://www.mtv.com/news/articles/1572107/20071017/index.jhtml.   143

10 M. Eugene Boring and Fred Craddock, *The People's New Testament Commentary* (Louisville: Westminster John Knox, 2004), 38.

11 Richard B. Hays, *First Corinthians* (Louisville: John Knox, 1997), 258–66.

12 J. K. Rowling, *Harry Potter and the Deathly Hallows* (New York: Scholastic, 2007), 759; "Rowling Explains Changing Last Word in Harry Potter," *AllDAY,* July 28, 2007, http://allday.msnbc.msn.com/archive/2007/07/28/295678.aspx.

13 See also Stephen Adams, "Philip Pullman Helps Understanding of Theology, Says Archbishop of Canterbury," *The Telegraph,* May 28, 2009, http://www.telegraph.co.uk/news/newstopics/religion/5400460/Philip-Pullman-helps-understanding-of-theology-says-Archbishop-of-Canterbury.html.

14 Gibbs, "J. K. Rowling." I should note that Lewis said more than once that he did not write *The Chronicles of Narnia* as an avenue to spread the faith; like Rowling, he said that he imagined images from the story first. Christian themes were only later embedded in that story because of his own Christian faith. See, e.g., C. S. Lewis, "Sometimes Fairy Stories May Say Best What's to Be Said," in *Of*

Other Worlds: Essays and Stories, ed. Walter Hooper (New York: Harcourt Brace & Jovanovich, 1966), 36.

15 Rowan Williams, *Grace and Necessity: Reflections on Art and Love* (London: Continuum, 2005), 99.

16 Williams, *Grace and Necessity*, 384.

17 John Polkinghorne, *The God of Hope and the End of the World* (New Haven: Yale University Press, 2002), 43.

18 C. S. Lewis, "Introduction,"in *Phantastes and Lilith*, by George MacDonald (Grand Rapids: Eerdmans, 1964), 10–11.

19 J. R. R. Tolkien, "On Fairy-Stories," in *Tales from the Perilous Realms* (Boston: Houghton Mifflin, 2008), 386.

20 Smietana, "The Gospel According to J. K. Rowling."

21 Rowling, *Deathly Hallows*, 739.

22 L'Engle, *Walking on Water*, 121.

23 Rowling, *Deathly Hallows*, 405.

24 Rowling, *Deathly Hallows*, 411.

25 "J. K. Rowling at the Royal Albert Hall, 26 June 2003," *Accio Quote!* http://www.accio-quote.org/articles/2003/0626-alberthall-fry.htm.

26 *Matthew 1–13*, Ancient Christian Commentary on Scripture, ed. Manlio Simonetti (Downer's Grove, Ill.: InterVarsity, 2001), 157.

27 "J. K. Rowling at the Royal Albert Hall," 26 June 2003, *Accio Quote!* http://www.accioquote.org/articles/2003/0626-alberthall-fry.htm.

28 Rowling, *Deathly Hallows*, 441.

29 J. K. Rowling, *Harry Potter and the Order of the Phoenix* (New York: Scholastic, 2003), 841.

30 J. K. Rowling, *Harry Potter and the Sorcerer's Stone* (New York: Scholastic, 1998), 257.

31 Rowling, *Order of the Phoenix*, 74.

32 Rowling, *Deathly Hallows*, 309.

33 Rowling, *Deathly Hallows*, 581.

34 Hans Urs von Balthasar, *A Theology of History* (1959; San Francisco: Ignatius, 1994).

35 Rowling, *Deathly Hallows*, 693.

36 Gibbs, "J. K. Rowling."

37 Weiss, "Christian Themes Abound in Potter."

38 Rowling, *Deathly Hallows*, 738.

39 Rowan Williams, *Tokens of Trust: An Introduction to Christian Belief* (Louisville: Westminster John Knox, 2007), 57.

40 Peter Abelard, "Exposition of the Epistle to the Romans," trans. Gerald E. Moffat, *A Scholastic Miscellany: Anselm to Ockham*, Library of Christian Classics 10 (Philadelphia: Westminster, 1956), 278.

41 Ken Cuthbertson, "The Christening of Harry Potter—Beyond a 'Mere'

Christianity," *Presbyterian Outlook*, July 27, 2007, http://www
.pres-outlook.com/reviews/book-reviews/5310.html.

42 Rowling, *Deathly Hallows*, 731.

43 N. T. Wright, *Simply Christian: Why Christianity Makes Sense*
(New York: HarperSanFrancisco, 2006), 116.

44 J. K. Rowling, *Harry Potter and the Prisoner of Azkaban* (New York:
Scholastic, 1999), 206–7.

45 Rowling, *Deathly Hallows*, 687.

46 Rowling, *Deathly Hallows*, 693.

47 Rowling, *Order of the Phoenix*, 838.

48 J. K. Rowling, *Harry Potter and the Goblet of Fire* (New York: Scholastic, 2000), 679.

49 Williams, *Tokens of Trust*, 62–63; Wright, *Simply Christian*, 10.

50 Rowling, *Order of the Phoenix*, 618–19.

51 Rowling, *Deathly Hallows*, 683.

52 Wright, *Simply Christian*, 126.

53 Rowan Williams, *On Christian Theology* (Malden, Mass.: Blackwell,
2000), 124.

54 Rowling, *Sorcerer's Stone*, 297.

55 J. K. Rowling, *Harry Potter and the Chamber of Secrets* (New York:
Scholastic, 1999), 333.

56 Rowling, *Deathly Hallows*, 722.

57 Rowling, *Deathly Hallows*, 747.

58 Rowling, *Order of the Phoenix*, 67.

59 Rowling, *Goblet of Fire*, 711.

60 Rowling, *Goblet of Fire*, 713.

61 Tertullian, *Apologeticum*, 39.

62 J. R. R. Tolkien, *The Letters of J. R. R. Tolkien*, ed. Humphrey Carpenter (1981; Boston: Houghton Mifflin, 2000), 100.

63 "J. K. Rowling Web Chat Transcript," *The Leaky Cauldron*, July
30, 2007, http://www.the-leaky-cauldron.org/2007/7/30/j-k-rowling
-web-chat-transcript.

64 Jonathan Petre, "J. K. Rowling: 'Christianity Inspired Harry Potter,'" *The Telegraph*, October 20, 2007, http://www.telegraph.co.uk
/culture/books/fictionreviews/3668658/J-K-Rowling-Christianity
-inspired-Harry-Potter.html.

65 Jürgen Moltmann, *The Coming of God: Christian Eschatology*, trans.
Margaret Kohl (Minneapolis: Fortress, 1996), 69.

66 N. T. Wright, *Surprised by Hope: Rethinking Heaven, the Resurrection, and the Mission of the Church* (New York: HarperOne, 2008),
12, 25.

67 Rowling, *Deathly Hallows*, 698.

145

68 Rowling, *Order of the Phoenix,* 816.
69 J. K. Rowling, *The Tales of Beedle the Bard* (New York: Scholastic, 2008), 79.
70 Wright, *Surprised by Hope,* 15.
71 Rowling, *Prisoner of Azkaban,* 392.
72 Wright, *Surprised by Hope,* 29.
73 John Gray, *Black Mass: Apocalyptic Religion and the Death of Utopia* (New York: Farrar, Straus & Giroux, 2007), 2.
74 Rowling, *Deathly Hallows,* 441.